UNLOCK YOU[R FAITH-LIFE]

*Unlock Your Faith-[Life], a collection] of inspiring articles se[lected by Norman Vincent] Peale, is a book which combines expert guidance with great stories of faith and achievement. More than forty true and unusual experiences from *Guideposts Magazine*, none of which has been published before in book form, have been selected for this volume for their apt illustrations of ten typical life situations with which most people are at some time or another confronted. These stories alone would make a stirring volume—but what makes this anthology unique is the addition of ten specially-written 'guides' by Norman Vincent Peale, whose *Power of Positive Thinking* and other best-selling books have inspired millions.

This is a book to be treasured and one to which the owner will often turn.

By the same author

THE TOUGH-MINDED OPTIMIST
THE AMAZING RESULTS OF POSITIVE THINKING
THE POWER OF POSITIVE THINKING
THE POSITIVE PRINCIPLE TODAY
THE POWER OF POSITIVE THINKING FOR YOUNG PEOPLE
INSPIRING MESSAGES FOR DAILY LIVING
STAY ALIVE ALL YOUR LIFE
A GUIDE TO CONFIDENT LIVING
ADVENTURES IN THE HOLYLAND
THE COMING OF THE KING
SIN, SEX AND SELF-CONTROL
JESUS OF NAZARETH
ENTHUSIASM MAKES THE DIFFERENCE
THE NEW ART OF LIVING
YOU CAN IF YOU THINK YOU CAN

In collaboration with Smiley Blanton, M.D.

THE ART OF REAL HAPPINESS
FAITH IS THE ANSWER

Edited by Norman Vincent Peale

GUIDEPOSTS
FAITH MADE THEM CHAMPIONS
UNLOCK YOUR FAITH-POWER

UNLOCK YOUR FAITH-POWER

Edited by
NORMAN VINCENT PEALE

CEDAR BOOKS
An imprint of William Heinemann Limited

Published by Cedar Books
an imprint of
William Heinemann Limited
10 Upper Grosvenor Street, London W1X 9PA
LONDON   MELBOURNE   TORONTO
JOHANNESBURG   AUCKLAND

Copyright 1957
by Guideposts Associates, Inc.
All rights reserved

First published by World's Work Ltd 1958
First published as a Cedar Book 1960
This impression 1986

0 434 11113 9

Printed in Great Britain by
Richard Clay (The Chaucer Press) I.td,
Bungay, Suffolk

Contents

1
OPEN THE DOOR TO GOD'S GUIDANCE

How You Can Find God's Guidance
by Catherine Marshall — 12

Appointment with Adventure
by Lowell Thomas, Jr. — 15

The Lights in the Halliday Home
by Mary Martin — 19

The Thunderous Power of Silence
by Stephen Thiermann — 23

2
BELIEVE YOUR FEARS AWAY

Ways to Find Your Secret Sanctuary
by Margaret Blair Johnstone — 28

Confessions of an Optimist
by Thomas B. Costain — 32

How Does a Man Face Fear?
by Harold R. Medina — 36

Life Without Marriage
by Anita Colby — 40

Be Bold . . . and mighty forces will come to your aid
by Arthur Gordon — 44

3
LOVE!

My Luminous Universe
by Helen Keller — 50

No One Is Alone
  by LORETTA YOUNG 54

How to Be a Lovable Person
  by SMILEY BLANTON 57

4
PUT YOUR DIFFICULTIES TO WORK

Poverty Never Made Us Poor
  by IVY BAKER PRIEST 62

My Favourite Thanksgiving Story
  by DOUGLAS MACARTHUR 66

Seeing-Eye People
  by CAROLE URICH 70

Ordeal By Water
  by MARILYN BELL 73

Our Different Gifts
  by PAUL ANDERSON 78

5
GIVE YOURSELF AWAY

What Is Tithing?
  by JOHN and ELIZABETH SHERRILL 84

Words I Live By
  by WILLIAM NICHOLS 89

Flames that Lick the Iron Curtain
  by ROBERT MONTGOMERY 91

Spiritual Commandos
  by LEE H. BRISTOL, JR. 94

Beauty Secret of a Plain Girl . . .
  by MURIEL SANATSAN 97

6
ACCEPT THE CHALLENGE OF YOUR CHURCH

Inside Our Home
by Mrs. Billy Graham — 100

How We Rediscovered Sunday
by Glenn Ford — 104

The Chain Around My Neck
by Jimmy Durante — 108

A Medal for Freddie
by Rosalind Russell — 113

7
EXPERIENCE THE JOY OF SELF-SURRENDER

The Crisis of Self-Surrender
by Samuel M. Shoemaker — 120

Decision of the Heart
by Bonnie Bonhiver — 124

24 Words that Can Change Your Life
by Herbert J. Taylor — 127

The Strength of Kanoh
by Stanley Manierre — 131

Discovery at Oak Ridge
by Len LeSourd — 134

8
LEARN THE LESSONS OF SPIRITUAL HEALING

A Minister Writes on the Power to Heal
by Alfred William Price — 140

A Doctor Examines the Power to Heal
by Omar John Fareed, M.D. — 145

A Reporter Looks at the Power to Heal
by Ruth Cranston — 149

I Saw It Happen
  by IVAN H. HAGEDORN   154
Opportunity in Work Clothes
  by HENRY J. KAISER, JR.   157

9

KNOW HOW TO FORGIVE OTHERS AND YOURSELF

My Father Held the Gun
  by MILTON J. COHEN   162
A Pickpocket Faces Tomorrow
  ANONYMOUS   166
The Boy Who Couldn't Face His Friends
  by CLIFF MILNOR   171
This Could Happen to You
  by CATHERINE CLARK   173

10

CHANGE YOUR LIFE THROUGH PRAYER

God, Send Someone!
  by DICK SULLIVAN   178
Research for a Prayer
  by PAUL DE KRUIF   183
The World Is Waiting
  by GENE LOCKHART   187

Here's How This Book Can Help You

EACH month *Guideposts Magazine* sends out to a cross section of our readers in the U.S.A. an editorial survey which includes this question: "What do you feel you need most in your own spiritual development?"

The overwhelming response: "More faith!"

Unlock Your Faith-Power is Guideposts' answer to the thousands of people who have expressed this wish. Strengthening faith can be done in a number of ways. We have carefully chosen ten methods—then selected forty-three articles from *Guideposts Magazine* which we feel direct readers along the most helpful and inspirational roads to increased faith.

I would like to make a few suggestions as to how you may benefit the most from this book. First, place it on the reading table by your bed, or at some other strategic place, where you can refer to it regularly. Look over the ten guides and decide which path you first want to take on your way to greater personal faith. Then, make up a definite reading plan. Limiting yourself to one article a day, for example, will give you time to absorb and reflect on what each author has to say to you. Follow up your reading with a plan of personal action in your home, at your place of work, at your church, in your community.

This book can be of special value to you in other ways. It is a rich source of material for devotionals or speeches. Many of the articles could be used for discussion purposes in Sunday School classes, Bible Study groups, Youth and

Adult Prayer Fellowships. Perhaps you know of a friend who is in particular need of an infusion of faith. This book is an ideal gift for the lonely, the bereaved and the shut-in.

But most of all, it offers to you an adventure in faith. We can give you the keys to the doors ahead. The rest is up to you.

Norman Vincent Peale

Open the Door to God's Guidance

"IF you are not sure you believe that God exists, or that He can possibly be interested in your little affairs," writes Catherine Marshall in one of the stories you are about to read, "then you are just the person to experiment with guidance."

Wise indeed is the person who comes to realise that he can never be a complete master of his own fate. This is God's world. Having created us, God is always ready to help us. *But first we must ask.*

When we ask, we are saying in effect that we want to be in tune with God's plan for us. God's guidance can then come to us in many ways. Through prayer and meditation. Through the wisdom we read in the Scriptures. Through other spiritual writings.

Mary Martin, for instance, tells how as a school girl she found guidance in a beloved spiritual motto. Lowell Thomas, Jr., and his wife describe how a poem which they pasted to the dashboard of their plane helped guide them through some fifty thousand miles of rigorous travel. There are stories here about individuals who found God's voice in silence. But the Master Key that unlocks the door to God's guidance is an open, receptive heart.

Norman Vincent Peale

How You Can Find God's Guidance
by CATHERINE MARSHALL

> *"When we put our lives into God's hands and ask Him to direct us, amazing results follow." The widow of beloved Peter Marshall writes about some of the beautiful personal discoveries she has made.*

I HAVE two women friends who own and operate a charming summer seaside inn, noted for its superb food. For the 1952 season they had planned to open the inn about 15th June. But two weeks before, letters began pouring in requesting earlier reservations. It scarcely seemed right to refuse so many would-be guests. There was not, however, enough help in the kitchen. On the morning before the guests were to arrive, they still lacked a pastry-cook and a dishwasher.

That morning one of the women (whom I'll call Beryl), rose early. A life-long Catholic, she knelt down by her bed and asked God for His help. Often in the past I have heard this friend pray. Her prayers are reverent, but very informal.

"I haven't the least idea where to find this help, Lord," she prayed. "This hotel is your business as well as mine. Will you please lead me to a dishwasher and a pastry-cook?"

Then she rose and began dressing. Her business partner awakened enough to ask anxiously, "What are you going to do now? Where are you going so early?"

"I don't know," was the astonishing reply, "but somehow I know God will show me."

Beryl got in her car and headed down the boulevard towards the business district. Half-way to town she saw two coloured men standing at a bus stop. On an impulse, she drew up to the kerb beside them. "I run a little hotel down the beach," she said, "and need some extra help. You men wouldn't be needing jobs, would you?"

Big grins appeared on the two men's faces. "Yes, ma'am, we do. We've been looking for jobs around here, and haven't found any. We were just starting back home to North Carolina."

"What can you do?" Beryl asked.

"Sam here, he's a first-rate pastry-cook. I'm a dish-washer."

"Climb in," said Beryl.

The two men stayed the entire season and proved to be the best help the inn had that year.

I well know how fantastic such guidance through circumstances may seem to people who have never had any similar experience. Yet it is this very dramatic quality, plus the juxtaposition of need and supply, which makes it difficult to tag such events 'mere coincidence'.

God used the guidance of circumstances in leading Peter Marshall, my husband, from Scotland to the United States to enter the ministry. Peter wanted to go to China. That door was shut in his face. He then wanted to go into home mission work in Scotland. That door closed too. The way to the United States opened. This last proved to be God's green light.

The reverse of this is that when we can get our own way only by riding roughshod over other people's lives and affairs, what we want is probably not right for us. Door-crashing and wire-pulling have little part in God's scheme of things. Circumstances work for us when we are on the right track.

Before the summer of 1944 the possibility of asking a Living Lord a direct question and receiving a specific answer had never once occurred to me.

But during that summer a crisis of illness emboldened me to take a leap of faith. I gave God a blank cheque with my life. Put most simply, this amounted to the willingness to take my marching orders from God for the rest of my life.

From the moment of that decision God's guidance became a personal reality. Everyday life lost its boredom and feeling of futility and became a series of exciting adventures.

If you are really serious about finding God's will in any particular, don't overlook the ground-work of self-surrender. Most of us think of our lives in compartmentalised fashion—business life, home life, etc.

Actually, life is of one piece. This fact makes it almost impossible for God to direct a man's business life, for example, when the man still insists on running his social contacts or some other part of his life in his own way.

Many humans fail in early experiments with guidance because they fear the blank cheque. Deeply ingrained is the idea that God wants to take away our fun. It is at this point that many people refuse to believe or trust the love of God for them. My own observation would prove that what God really wants for each of us is joy, health, productivity in our jobs, wonderful friends, and fulfilled, integrated personalities.

God has dared to give His creatures free will; He regards as sacred this freedom to choose. From experience I know that when I grow stubborn, plant my feet firmly in the earth like a Missouri mule, and insist on my own way, God builds no fires under my mulish disposition. He just waits patiently until I see the error of my ways. But in the mulish interlude, no direction comes.

Abraham Lincoln once said, "I am satisfied that when the Almighty wants me to do, or not to do, any particular thing, He finds a way of letting me know it." That's exactly the point.

Having experimented with guidance for the last ten years, I have found when we really want God to direct our decisions, He will find a way to do so. Since my husband's death in 1949, a series of major decisions were inevitable for me. For many of these I was poorly qualified, with little basic knowledge or know-how. In at least three instances, the wrong choice would have altered completely the channel and direction of my life. Yet with God's help, in each case I was prevented from making those wrong turnings.

But if we ever wonder whether we are subconsciously mistaking our will for God's will, we can easily test our decision against the other avenues of guidance: the Bible, direct communication through the inner Voice, our friends, or a combination of all of these. But in the end, with our co-operation, He *does* succeed in keeping us on the right path.

If you are one of these individuals who is not even sure you believe that God exists, or at best, that He can possibly be interested in your little affairs, then you are just the person to experiment with guidance. The stuff of our everyday life lends itself beautifully to this kind of experimentation. A few personal experiences of finding God's wisdom, a wisdom easily recognised as beyond your own, a few proofs of His amazing personal solicitude, and your doubts, too, will melt away.

But you'll never know unless you try it.

Appointment with Adventure
by LOWELL THOMAS, JR.

Strange lands and strange people are visited by a young American couple. The journey was often rugged, sometimes dangerous, but there was always an unseen guide.

IN 1954 my wife, Tay, and I did something we had always dreamed of: we took a light plane and spent twelve months visiting the most out-of-the-way places we could find in Asia, in the Middle East, and in Africa.

In our single-engined Cessna, affectionately dubbed 'Charlie', we flew some 50,000 miles. We walked for days with bearded Afghan nomads. We talked with the happy, uninhibited Pygmies of the Congo. We flew over the snow-crowned peak of Kilimanjaro. We sailed in a primitive *dhow* on the Persian Gulf. And we went to the Emperor of Abyssinia's birthday ball.

Today, as we talk over our experiences, a little poem flashes into my mind, a poem Tay found somewhere and pasted on the dashboard of our plane. I don't know who wrote it, but it semed to express our attitude perfectly:

> "Peace be in thy home
>   And in thy heart.
> Or if thou roam
>   Earth's highways wide,
> The Lord be at they side,
>   To bless and guide."

Earth's highways wide . . . We were, indeed, roaming them, and we did need a guide. With those six lines of verse pasted in front of us, we always felt we had one: a kindly, all-powerful Protector, into whose mighty hand we committed ourselves before the journey and Who, we truly believe, watched over us night and day.

We had faith in God's protection and guidance. And we needed other kinds of faith, too. Faith in the basic friendliness of people everywhere. Faith in our ability to 'take it', no matter how rough the going might be—and at times it was rugged.

Many of the people we met were aghast when they learned we were flying a single-engined plane, often in areas where there were no weather reports, no navigational aids of any kind. I had been a pilot since World War II, and Tay could handle the control if she had to. I was always pretty optimistic about everything. Tay was definitely on the conservative side. So we made a fairly well-balanced team. Even so, once or twice we did get into trouble.

Coming up from Damascus to Istanbul, on one occasion, I counted (optimistically) on a radio beacon that simply wasn't there. As a result, I got lost above a heavy overcast. Night fell, a wind-shift began pushing me far to the west, and petrol began running low.

Tay wasn't with me on this flight; she was grounded temporarily by an ear infection. I had a friend along, a mechanic, who got quieter and quieter as he watched the petrol gauge sink minute by minute. My radio compass, which on various other occasions had performed very badly, indicated one course. All my instincts indicated another. I finally decided to trust the compass. It guided us to Istanbul, all right, but we ran out of petrol approaching the airfield. My friend said calmly, "Are we going to make it, Lowell?" And I said, "I don't think so."

With our flaps down, and no power, we were dropping fast. I switched to the other petrol tank—long since empty—hoping to find a drop or two. The engine coughed twice, and that extra boost just pulled us on to the runway.

". . . The Lord be at thy side,
To bless and guide."

Some of our most interesting experiences came when we flew down into Africa. We stopped in Kenya, then pushed on to the Congo where we visited Anne Putnam, a remarkable American who has spent years among the Pygmies.

The Pygmies themselves are fascinating, happy-go-lucky little people, who reminded us at times of Disney's droll dwarfs. They make excellent parents, giving a baby all the love and indulgence it could possibly want—until a new baby comes along. Then the older child is treated almost as a grown-up, is given chores to do, and has to pull his weight in the family boat. The result is a group of remarkably well-adjusted children.

We offered to take various Pygmies for a ride in 'Charlie',

our aeroplane, but only one had the courage to accept. This was a little fellow who had killed an elephant by himself, with only a spear, and he was the bravest Pygmy around.

Anne Putnam asked him later if the flight in our plane had frighened him. He said no, that he had 'tied up his spirit', a graphic way of saying that he had kept his nerve.

In the tremendous mountains of northern Pakistan, for instance, we organised a donkey caravan of our own to visit a remote valley in the Karakoram range. It took us four days to get there over the roughest track I have ever seen—even worse than the trail to Lhasa, Tibet, that I followed with my father in 1949. At times it was just a narrow ledge skirting precipices 2,000 feet high. We struggled along, 17 or 18 miles a day, living on yak meat and *ghee*.[1]

It was while we were resting up in the valley that Tay discovered she was going to have a baby. For five years we had been hoping for a child. Now we were worried. Overexertion could bring on a miscarriage, and here we were facing the nightmare ride back out. This was truly a time when we had to 'tie up our spirits', which we did by tying them up to God through prayer. We are both sure this helped us keep our nerve and get out safely. The baby, Anne, arrived very satisfactorily in August, 1955.

There are many such memories we are trying to put into a book we are writing. And what do they all add up to, really?

Our purpose, basically, was to learn what we could about the more obscure peoples of this planet and to report our findings—on the theory that the more knowledge there is of other lands, the less misunderstanding there will be, and the greater the chances for world peace.

Of all the things we learned, the most important, I think, was this: that the world is *not* a hostile place. Everywhere we went, people reacted to honesty with

[1] Native butter.

honesty. They responded to friendliness with more friendliness, to little acts of kindness with larger acts of kindness. These are Christian virtues, but they are also universal human traits. We found them everywhere.

We are only a couple of young Americans, not too wise in matters of statecraft, perhaps. But this adventure of ours left us believing that in the love and understanding which Christ taught us lies the only hope for a peaceful world.

A new commandment I give unto you, that ye love one another . . .[1] In our own small way, we tried to follow that commandment.

The Lights in the Halliday Home

by MARY MARTIN

> *A famous actress reveals how she came by a proverb and a creed—both of which now illuminate her private and public life.*

SHORTLY after we were married, my husband, Richard Halliday, was rummaging through some old papers and keepsakes of mine when he came upon a yellowed card, and on it, in the scrawl of a schoolgirl, was written:

"I would be true, for there are those who trust me; I would be pure, for there are those who care; I would be strong, for there is much to suffer; I would be brave, for there is much to dare; I would be a friend to all—the foe—the friendless; I would be giving, and forget the gift; I would be humble, for I know my weakness; I would look up—and laugh—and love—and lift."

On the other side of the card was a faded violet, and a note in the same childish scrawl:

"Mrs. Alvis read this poem to us girls today, and I hope my Heavenly Father will always let me live by this creed."

[1] John 13. 34.

Mrs. Alvis was my teacher in Weatherford Junior High in Texas.

As soon as he found it, Richard framed the creed in a glass panel, so that the words on one side, and my prayer to abide by them on the other, could both be visible. It is on a table in the library of our home in Connecticut, where it is always seen and often read aloud.

Some years ago I was rehearsing a play called *Lute Song*, which had a Chinese setting. Richard, doing some research on the background of *Lute Song*, found this ancient, anonymous proverb:

"If there is righteousness in the heart, there will be beauty in the character. If there be beauty in the character, there will be harmony in the family home. If there is harmony in the home, there will be order in the nation. When there is order in the nation, there will be peace in the world."

The proverb is embroidered in a petit-point rug, which my husband designed for our living-room. It took me over three years to make the rug. But I did. In the rug is also a view of our home in winter; the cherry tree in the yard which our daughter, Heller, loves so much; a figure of Heller when she was five and acting and travelling with us in *Annie Get Your Gun*, because we wanted her with us; and my son Larry's field of yellow mustards and red roses, and his favourite guitar. In one corner are a pair of clasped hands: mine and Richard's.

The creed and proverb are the real lights in the Halliday home; the lights we try to live by.

All the parents I know, including myself, face the frightening and frustrating feeling of losing all contact with their children when they are in their teens. At 17 Larry came home on a school holiday and got our permission to attend a card party with his friends in New York City. At 2.00 a.m. he had not returned. The next hour was an agony. At 3.00 a.m. he phoned and said:

"I didn't realise it was so late because we were having

such a good time. We're in this girl's apartment." He gave us the phone number and address, and added, "I'm not doing anything you'd be ashamed of."

"I would be true, for there are those who trust me . . ."

While Larry was in the Air Force in England two years ago, he married a girl with the lovely name of Maj. She's Swedish and a dress designer in London, and she wrote us a full description of their wedding in a Swedish church in London.

"You would have been terribly proud of your son," she said. "When he discovered I had only a Swedish Bible, he gave me an English one. He doesn't read Swedish."

Larry's letters are amazing and wonderful because he's pouring back all the things now we thought we could never teach him: "I'm beginning to understand all the anxious moments I've caused you and Richard," he writes, "and all your problems and hopes."

"If there is righteousness in the heart, there will be beauty in the character . . ."

Heller is beginning to pour back the things we never thought we could teach her either. For instance, during the Los Angeles run of *Peter Pan*, our most exciting venture, Heller cracked her toes badly while playing one afternoon. But she performed that night and every night after, acting, singing, and dancing, and we never knew about her cracked toes until much later.

"I would be a friend to all—the foe—the friendless; I would be giving, and forget the gift; I would be humble, for I know my weakness; I would look up—and laugh—and love—and lift."

When I needed them most, such thoughts have given me strength beyond endurance. There have been times during the 276 performances of *Peter Pan* when I had a bad attack of flu (on a matinee day too), several colds which were doctored in the wings to give me sufficient voice to sing, and emergency treatment after I flew head-on into a wall.

For those who do not know *Peter Pan*, that incredible, but real, boy does a lot of flying from Neverland to our land. An invisible wire is attached to my back and controlled by experts behind the scenes. But even the best of mechanical devices sometime fails. It is amazing that they fail so rarely. Anyway, in San Francisco I flew into the wall and tore all the ligaments on my left side. Worried doctors agreed: "You can't function. Don't try."

But thousands of children were expecting to see Peter Pan, we just couldn't disappoint them. With many novocaine injections, I went on.

"I would be brave, for there is much to dare . . ."

After that accident there was nothing to fear except fear. But my creed and proverb forbid it . . . just as they forbid ugliness or pettiness or anger.

I had occasion to read the creed on television once and a few days later received this letter from a minister in Wilmington, Delaware:

"The creed you quoted, 'I would Be True', was written by Howard Walter, a colleague of mine during the first World War. The last time I saw him was in Bombay in August, 1918. He had come to India to work, in spite of the doctor's warning that the condition of his heart and lungs was such that his chances of survival were very poor.

"One morning he read me a telegram that had just come from his wife, saying that she and the children were down with severe cases of the flu in Lahore. Howard said: 'I must go to Lahore at once. There is no doctor or nurse available in that city, and all are down with this awful disease.' Two days later I received word of his death from flu.

"We loved him greatly. His influence in India was quite wonderful. Your reading his poem is evidence that it still continues."

Things never die, do they? A timeless link is forged with the lovely words and thoughts written by a missionary in

India, a friend in Wilmington who cannot forget him, and a schoolgirl in Texas who loved the teacher for the sake of the creed she taught.

The Thunderous Power of Silence
by STEPHEN THIERMANN

> *Over 300 years ago the Quakers learned a way to guidance, which, when followed, can be not only effective, but often highly dramatic.*

IN 1938 three members of the religious Society of Friends (Quakers) walked boldly into the Berlin Gestapo office of Reinhard Heydrich, Himmler's deputy chief. They asked Heydrich for two specific changes in regulations, which would allow them to take persecuted Jews out of Germany.

Heydrich studied the proposal coldly for a moment, then asked the visitors to wait in an adjoining room. One of the petitioners, the late Rufus Jones, reported later that, as in the Quaker custom, he and his associates used the time for silent prayer and meditation.

It didn't occur to them that the ante-room was undoubtedly wired and that their silence might have had an unexpected effect outside the room. No one knows exactly what did happen, only that their silence was broken after about half an hour by the dramatic statement:

"Your requests have been granted."

Soon after, announcement of the changes in Gestapo regulations was broadcast throughout Germany, and many persecuted Jews were released.

The Quakers first discovered, over 300 years ago, the thunderous power of silence. Not every experience with silence can be as dramatic as the one in the Gestapo headquarters, but there are many less spectacular opportunities to use silence in everyday life situations.

Heading off Trouble: Far too often word-sparks escape from us and ignite trouble: a clash at a picket line, a bitter exchange between parents, or a feud in the accounting department. A few minutes of silence might have prevented all these ugly situations.

Surging crowds once gathered around a woman taken in adultery. Angry voices challenged Jesus to side either with the woman or with those who sought to stone her. Instead of speaking, Jesus calmly bent down and scribbled with his finger on the ground. After emotions had a chance to cool, Jesus was able to talk to the crowd effectively about love and understanding.

Today the same principle is applied to industrial disputes in the well-known 'cooling-off' period of labour negotiations. Ever try a 'cooling-off' period in your personal life? When tempted to let words-spark fly, I remember the words of the great American humourist Josh Billings:

"Silence is one of the hardest arguments to refute."

Better communication: Author-housewife May Richstone, because she was threatened with a throat operation, was forced to keep silent for six weeks. At first she was worried she would become a dull companion, but her husband laughed playfully when he heard the news:

"Every man I know will be jealous of me."

But before the six weeks' silence was over, Mrs. Richstone found herself reporting:

"Wit is refreshing, profound perorations are admirable, eloquence is an art. But for daily living, silence tops them all."

A nineteenth-century English author, Sydney Smith discovered the same basic lesson. Speaking of his friend, the historian Thomas Macaulay, Smith said:

"He has occasional flashes of silence which make his conversation perfectly delightful."

Even public speakers have found silence a most effective technique. Quakers at a Chappaqua, New York, Meeting tell the story of a speech given by one of the senior editors of the *Reader's Digest*, Charles Ferguson. When allotted a half-hour, Mr. Ferguson divided the time alternately into talk and silence: he spoke five minutes, then asked the meeting to consider his point in silence for the next five minutes before going on to another point.

And prayer, our communication with God, can also be vastly improved by the careful use of silence. Prayer is too often a monologue—a gush of thoughts, petitions, even thanks. The quality of these talks with God is greatly improved if sprinkled liberally with periods of silence.

Problem Solving: Inspiration rarely comes to the talkative. A period of relaxed silence can help us find answers to many problems.

Haydn, the composer, declared, "When my work does not advance, I retire into the chapel and immediately ideas come."

From the time of Archimedes (who discovered the law of specific gravity while relaxing in silence in his bath) to the present, scientists have deliberately used periods of relaxed silence for problem solving.

One day when he was emotionally upset, Galileo went into the cathedral at Pisa to calm himself. Seated in the centre of the nave with his head bowed in silence, he saw out of the corner of his eye, the slow, measured, to-and-fro movement of the large chandeliers. Quietly he studied the arcs which were formed and discovered the important principle of the pendulum—a discovery that might never have been made if Galileo had not practised creative silence.

Achieving Peace of Mind: One of the most important of all uses of silence is in renewing the mind and spirit. "At the heart of the cyclone tearing the sky is a place of central calm," said Edwin Markham. Great power comes from calm sources.

Nobel Prize winner André Gide, describing a journey to the Belgian Congo tells how, after a forced march of several days, his native bearers refused to go on. The bearers said they'd travelled so fast their spirits were left behind. They were going to stay in camp until their spirits caught up.

The aimless busyness of our lives often is the result of having outrun our spiritual resources. A few minutes set aside from the rush of office, factory or household for periods of silence can do much towards allowing these resources to catch up again.

In using silence to renew our mind or spirit, two problems will trouble us: the difficulty of finding time to spare, and of floundering around in silence.

Hard as it is to find even five minutes for silent withdrawal, it is important to create the time regularly somewhere in each day. This is particularly true at the beginning of experiments with silence. Psychologists tell us that to let exceptions occur in beginning a new habit is like dropping a ball of string which has just been carefully wound; only a great many turns can compensate for the single slip.

The second danger, floundering in silence, can be reduced by scheduling silence early in the day before we are barraged by the opinions, ideas, and demands of other people.

Silence is a difficult habit to obtain, but with practise in the art, you will find great rewards. It pays, surely, to increase your word power, but you may find that it pays even more to increase your silence power.

Believe Your Fears Away

No one can live a successful life if he is beset by fear and frustration. Fear nibbles away at strength. Frustration drains away energy. How, then, do we meet our fears and vanquish them? How do we find relief from frustration?

The people represented in the following pages have found, through their own experience, an answer to these subtle but devastating anxieties. Each has a different problem and a different method of solution. But you will recognise a basic theme coursing through all of them. That theme is Belief. Faith.

Perhaps your nerves are on edge and you are not sure of just what it is you fear. You are not alone. God can help you. When fear begins to surround you, repeat this text: *The Lord is my helper, I will not be afraid; what can man do to me?*[1]

Finally, there is the story whose very title might change your life. It has the ring of victory and triumph—'Be Bold —and Mighty Forces Will Come to Your Aid.'

Norman Vincent Peale

Hebrews 13. 6.

Ways to Find Your Secret Sanctuary
by MARGARET BLAIR JOHNSTONE

> Where can one find a refuge from cares and worries, where can one replenish his faith and confidence? The woman pastor of the Union Congregational Church of Groton, Massachusetts, tells how to find this sanctuary and this 'power to face life on lifted wings'.

WHAT is sanctuary? The dictionary defines it as a place of refuge, sacred and inviolable. Because of this, many of us think that to seek sanctuary in time of trouble is to take cowardly flight from reality. But it is not that. Rather it is flight *to* reality. It is when life's violence threatens and we do not seek sanctuary that we become escapists, dodging anxieties and scurrying among confusions. Like sparrows crossing a motorway by hopping, we do not realise that we have both the means and the power to rise above the danger coming at us from all sides.

Sanctuary is, essentially, a means of finding the power to face life on lifted wings. It is this power which the Unknown Prophet in Isaiah tells us enables men to "renew their strength . . . mount up with wings as eagles . . . run and not be weary . . . walk and not faint."

All of us have access to this power. Sooner or later, that which is weak in us runs crying to lay down some burden on Someone stronger. When that Someone stronger gives us strength to pick up our burden and bear it triumphantly ourselves, then have we found sanctuary.

We need not turn to some enchanted island, remote from daily living, to find our place of refuge. One of the most misinterpreted verses in the Bible is the familiar, *He*

This article appeared simultaneously in *Reader's Digest* and *Guideposts Magazine*.

leadeth me beside the still waters; He restoreth my soul.[1]
Most of us think the still waters were placid lakes or quiet meadow brooks. But not so! They were part of torrential mountain streams where day in and out the shepherd had to lead his flock. But there each day he managed to find some 'waters of quietness', some pool of still water spilled alongside but fed by and part of the fierce mainstream. And we too can find, right alongside life's mainstream, the still waters which will renew our minds.

From earliest times man has been told exactly where to find and how to seek sanctuary. God gave Moses one set of directions when He said, *Put off thy shoes from off thy feet, for the place whereon thou standest is holy ground.*[2] Yet how many of us go blindly by Nature's sanctuary places!

Do you need sanctuary? Then look in your own backyard. Ever since Eden some men have come nearer God's heart in a garden than anywhere else on earth. On your own patch of holy ground you may find renewal. A student pointed out that the decisive element on the discovery of the law of gravitation was not so much the apple as the garden. Newton was alone in the quiet of a garden when he saw his great truth.

The mountains and the sea are perennial sanctuary places to which you may turn aside at any time, even by proxy. "When things get thick I turn my back on my busy kitchen and gaze at the mountain scene framed by my window," says a mother fortunate enough to be able to lift up her eyes into real hills. But a professor I know has no such view. So he has hung a colour transparency of the sea in the east window of his city apartment, and this he sees on waking each day.

But perhaps you are not too keen on Nature and God-created sanctums. For all His love of Nature, Jesus knew there was a time when you would have to go into your room and shut the door. And when He said, *Come ye your-*

---

[1] *Psalms* 23. 2, 3.   [2] *Exodus* 3. 5.

selves apart into a desert place, and rest a while,[1] He was pointing out not only the place, but the way to reach sanctuary.

I have a friend who is a social worker in a slum. She lives in a settlement house. Her single window looks out on an alley littered with garbage and filth. Her life is an endless process of dirty pavement pounding, tenement stair climbing, grievance hearing and monotonous record keeping. One night I paused at her door to leave a message. She invited me in. I found her small dingy room aglow with candlelight. "This is how I keep my sanity," she explained. "Every night, no matter how late it is, for 15 minutes I light all these candles. To me the most serene thing on earth is a lighted candle."

You may find sanctuary even in the lunch hour. Music can recharge you when you are mentally beaten or nervously exhausted. You say you don't have time for concerts? Well, then, what about a record booth? "I take 20 minutes for lunch and the rest for feasting my ears on Brahms," says an editor who, despite a crammed office, never seems pushed. Her musical sanctuary sends her back to her appointments on lifted wings.

You can find sanctuary in your bath-tub! The next time life crowds you, try immersing yourself in a tub of warm water. One of the oldest of all sanctuary rites is ablution : the ceremonial washing away of life's soil and stain. One of the newer healing techniques is hydrotherapy : the scientific purging of tension and pain.

And don't forget the old rocking chair. A woman who reared a large family and ran a boarding house was asked how she remained so calm and composed. "Well," she said, "you know that big rocking chair up in my room? Every afternoon, no matter how busy I am, I go up there to rock awhile and empty out my brains."

Sometimes, however, we need to empty out more than our brains. You may find sanctuary where you empty out

[1] *Mark* 6. 31.

your soul. You can find it in a vacational shrine or on a business trip—by slipping into some Meditation Chapel like that in New York's Biltmore Hotel.

You may discover it kneeling in a hospital chapel praying for a dear one, or on the high seas—on a troopship or in the miniature cathedral aboard the *Ile de France*. You may find the Someone who 'keeps your going out and your coming in' by stopping at your own church before facing the humdrum of a busy work-day. Or you may touch Him in some shrine like that at Boston's Logan Field before the take-off into some unknown.

However, there comes times to all of us, and at all times there are some of us for whom no holy ground in Nature, no lonely place apart, no sanctum of man gives sanctuary, no matter how desperate our need.

Then what?

When disaster strikes on Royal Navy vessels, they instantly blow 'The Still'. It means: "Prepare to do the wise thing."

When the signal is piped, few men know the wise thing. But in the moments of enforced calm they find it. Each man calculates position and checks resources. By observing 'The Still' they rout confusion and frequently avert catastrophe.

So with our personal emergencies. Few of us instantly know the wise thing. "If only I could *know* what to do!" we cry, forgetting that the order of procedure is: *"Be still and know . . ."*

No matter how little you *know*, or even how little you think you have faith to believe, the next time you need sanctuary: *be still!* Stop instantly all feverish activity and do what those around you who have found sanctuary are doing.

A scientist, plagued by debts, a chronic illness, and a nagging family, once sought a shrine not too devoutly, but desperately. He could not believe what a friend told him: that if he repeated a prayer 13 times over and *then* asked for the desire of his heart, he would get it. But he had tried everything else and failed, so in a what-have-I-got-to-lose mood he started the prayer.

And, as he prayed, he began to think. What should I ask for if this were not humbug: Money? Health? Over and over he said the prayer. What was his heart's deepest yearning, he wondered. A happy home? Solvency? Thirteen times he said the prayer, then suddenly welling up from some hidden recess of him came the cry, "O God, I beg you, enlighten my mind and let me invent something very great to further human knowledge!" Amazed, he kept kneeling in the silence. So this was his desire of desires! Knowing it at last, Galileo rose to his feet, and went forth from his sanctuary and began the experiments which led to the invention of the telescope.

You may not find it is enough 'to go into your room and shut the door and pray,' however fervently. You may have to go out and open some door of life and serve. The next time you are hounded by fear or stymied by despair, go to your local hospital ward. You say you can't talk to sick folks? Very well, just take a bouquet of flowers and leave it there. Or stop in on that housebound old man across the street. You say you can't make him hear a thing? What of it? He eats, doesn't he? Take him a bowl of hot soup.

Sanctuary is where you find it. You can find it where you are, in your town, on your street, in your own heart.

Confessions of an Optimist

by THOMAS B. COSTAIN

> *A best-selling author describes with wit and logic how optimism in its purest phase is a noble form of courage and faith.*

I AM an optimist. I am sure that all the adjectives which usually are inserted before that word, such as 'foolish', 'rash', and even 'rank', can be applied to me. I have taken many a leap before allowing myself a good look; and, although I have had my falls, most of the plunges have turned out well.

I have little respect for Slow-and-Steady as a winner of races; certainly the tortoise would never have won if the hare had not been a silly, amateur show-off. Finally, and this is where the aforementioned adjectives lose all meaning, I am unreservedly and blissfully convinced that some, at least, of the finer things in life are as such as death and taxes.

Most people incline to the other way of looking at things. This must be so, because otherwise all the proverbs, wise saws, and axioms dinned into us from childhood would not be so solidly lined up on the side of slowness, steadiness, caution, saving, suspicion, and abhorrence of chances. If it were not so, we would not have been beset by anxious parents, lugubrious uncles, and harping teachers. I have been aware all my life that those who accept the philosophy of optimism are rather looked down upon and considered dangerous fellows while the pessimist, good old Slow-and-Steady, is respected as a solid citizen and the backbone of society. It is not my intention to argue the case for the one point of view against the other. Both kinds of people are needed; both play their parts in maintaining the necessary balance. I have no other purpose than to assert that I belong in the one class, the smaller and less respected, and that I am happy, and I think lucky, to be an optimist.

Of course, we foolish and rash fellows, we plungers-in-where-angels-fear-to-tread (if angels know fear, then courage must be ruled a myth), find that there are drawbacks to our way of looking at things. I have always been able to make money, but I have little sense as to what should be done with it. I often wonder just why this should be so, and where I have been at fault. It's rather like the riddle of the hen and the egg. If I had a sense of caution and an instinct for barricading myself against adverse winds, I might possibly be in a better financial position today. But on the other hand, would there have been anything to conserve if I had been canny and fearful of the future?

I have been an optimist for seventy years. I suppose I was born one. I haven't changed although there have been times when there seemed little to be optimistic about. A year ago I celebrated my seventieth birthday, and it proved a most pleasant day, without any misgivings or repinings or grumblings. In the morning I had looked into a bathroom mirror and had said to myself, "Seventy years old and don't yet look a day over eighty," but the members of my family and my friends assured me rather vehemently that I did not look my age. If they are right—and I hope they are—it is due in part at least to my having kept a cheerful outlook.

I get out of bed every morning at six o'clock; by seven, I find myself seated at my desk. I have done a good day's work by eleven-thirty or twelve. By noon the stream of invention is growing thin. I have put perhaps 2,500 words down on paper. That may seem small, but when you consider that I do this every day, the yearly outlook begins to loom large. I seldom attempt to write in the afternoons, which I devote to correspondence, reading and planning, and sometimes, of course, to such pleasant diversions as baseball games and movies.

Perhaps I should have explained earlier that I am not one of those who can remain cheerful while the house burns down or an epidemic is sweeping the neighbourhood. I worry, secretly, about trifles like an unkind letter, a thoughtless word. I realise all through these little downward dips in mood that they are of no consequence, that I am foolish to indulge in them, and that I will be through with them in an hour or two; but they go on occurring, and I can do nothing about them.

I am convinced that all writers are optimists whether they concede the point or not. This applies even to those who produce stark and grimly realistic work. How otherwise could any human being sit down before a pile of blank sheets and decide to write, say, 200,000 words on a given theme?

I know that all of my essays into print have needed the impetus of a strong form of blind faith. This was particularly true of *The Silver Chalice*. It was clear to me from the beginning that the story in my mind would consume a quarter million words in the telling. I knew that no amount of effort would yield much authentic material about certain important phases. Never has a period been so ardently searched and researched and voluminously written about with such small rewards in the way of proven fact. The Bible tells us about John the Apostle, but what is known about John the man? Who can say how the people lived in the Valley of the Cheesemakers and how justice was administered in Antioch? It is, moreover, a time which, rightly, is held sacred. A careless word can give deep offence, and it is impossible to please all the races and widely differing creeds.

It seemed to me certain also that the book which would result from my efforts would be woefully short of the transcendant story which filled my mind.

The completed book has been both criticised and praised. In spite of my own conviction that I should have made a better book of it, I am happy that I allowed myself to be persuaded into doing it by my optimistic promptings. The letters I have received, which have come from all over the world, in most cases have said that the writers had been helped by the book and strengthened in their faith.

I am proud that optimism dwells in me in some degree because in its highest and purest phrase it is a form of courage and faith. It has inspired great leaders, and it has sent men out on the long trails of exploration and adventure. It has kept scientists to their seemingly hopeless tasks, and it has been a candle in the murk of doubt in which the inventor exists. It lightens the task of the humble as well as the labours of the great.

It has been reported, and I think accurately, that on a certain dark day in the first year of the second world war, it devolved on Winston Churchill to inform the members of his Cabinet that France had been compelled to ask terms of the German invaders. The head of the British Government looked down the table at the far from cheerful faces of his colleagues.

"Gentlemen," he said, "we now stand alone. And I may say that I find it inspiring."

It is at such moments that optimism achieves a height where it is the noblest form of courage and a proof of undying faith.

How Does a Man Face Fear

by HAROLD R. MEDINA

> *Acrophobia is a fear of high places, a fear which affects many people as it did this famous judge. Here is an unusual recorded interview with Harold R. Medina, United States Court of Appeals, New York.*

IN 1940, eleven top U.S. Communists were sentenced by the court to terms in jail. The charge was conspiracy to overthrow the government by violence. Presiding judge at trial was Harold R. Medina, whose skill and patience during the long nine months were widely heralded and admired.

But there is a little known story behind that story. To get this account, a *Guideposts* reporter went to Judge Medina's office in New York City. A tape recorder was used in the interview, parts of which are presented here.

REPORTER: . . . and I read a lot about you, of course.

One thing interested me most: this little item about your fear of height.

(*Reporter hands the one-paragraph items to Judge Medina.*)

MEDINA: My acrophobia?

REPORTER: You're over it now, I suppose.

MEDINA: Oh, yes. Yes, I haven't had trouble with that for two, three years now.

REPORTER: But during the trial your fear was used against you. Would you be willing to tell about it?

(*For a moment Medina's face clouds—not quite in annoyance, more in reluctance to retrace a painful experience. Then he smiles.*)

MEDINA: These matters are a bit personal, you know. And there's nothing too unusual to tell. A lot of people have fear of height.

REPORTER: It might help them, knowing what you went through.

MEDINA: Perhaps.

(*Briefly, Judge Medina stares at the row of law books that line his office walls. Then when he speaks, it is in broken phrases.*)

Up until the trial, it was mostly a childhood fear. I knew it often then. I remember one summer, when I was a boy on Long Island, my father took me up to Niagara Falls. I could hear the roar as we came close to the falls. I saw a lot of people up ahead, standing at the rail, looking down at the water as it fell. I held my breath. I just couldn't go near the edge. I was afraid I would jump. Doesn't make much sense, but a thing like this never does.

REPORTER: And the fear came alive again during the trial?

MEDINA: Not right away. Soon after the trial started, I began to realise the defendants seemed more interested in spreading Communist propaganda, or in breaking up the trial, than they were in working for an acquittal. They wanted a mis-trial. They could succeed in two ways. Either by creating such disorder that I'd have to declare a mistrial; or by wrecking me personally. For the first five months of the trial, witnesses were truculent, attorneys were insolent; we had the greatest trouble keeping order in the court.

REPORTER: And then they started working on your fear of falling?

(*Judge Medina points towards the window. His large office is on the 22nd floor of the skyscraper court-house.*)

MEDINA: That's Foley Square, out front there. In the newspaper one day I saw a picture of the square. There were a lot of pickets marching up and down. They were carrying signs. 'Medina will fall like Forrestal'. It was just a few weeks after Defence Secretary James Forrestal had plunged to his death from a hospital window. That was the start of it. Then the chants began. "Medina will fall like Forrestal." The pickets chanted that all day down there in the street. Somehow they had learned about my fear of falling.

REPORTER: How long did this last?

MEDINA: I don't know. It seemed like months. I began to find the words *jump* and *fall* in messages. In my mail. In phone calls. I could feel the old acrophobia coming back.

(*Judge Medina moves in his chair, a bit uneasily.*)

REPORTER: How does a person solve a fear like this?

MEDINA: Ah. There you are. When I was a boy I just avoided high places. But how does a man face a fear that he can't avoid? I'll tell you the answer. In addition to the self-discipline, I had something else . . . prayer.

REPORTER: Prayer?

MEDINA: I don't mean a prayer directed only towards my fear of falling. I didn't suddenly say, "Now, Lord, you have got to take away my acrophobia." I mean a whole prayer-life that asked for strength and guidance in *all* that I was doing.

It was prayer that I had been building since I was a boy.

I was fortunate. I had prayer from the time I was a child, when my mother knelt with me at bedtime to read from her Episcopal Book of Common Prayer. I inherited not just a Sunday kind of prayer, but a daily, often hourly kind of prayer. I prayed constantly, on and off throughout the day, any time when I was thankful, or under stress, or when I was in any kind of trouble.

REPORTER: And prayer helped here?

MEDINA: Let me put it this way. It was prayer alone that kept me going during the sixth and seventh months of the trial. Right up to the moment in August, just before the trial ended, when I finally did collapse.

That was during the eighth month. There was no way of knowing then that everything would be over in a matter of weeks. At the time, I could see nothing ahead but endless days of bickering.

One day my head suddenly began to spin.

I recessed the court and walked quickly to the little room at the back of the court and I lay down. I felt almost panicky ... I sensed that this was a crisis. A turning. One road led to defeat; the other to victory. If I could not force myself to go back there I would be conquered. Not only would the trial be a failure, but personally I would be unable to be in control of myself.

(*Judge Medina leans forward and speaks in a lower tone.*)

I don't mind telling you I did a lot of praying in that little room. I prayed for strength and I prayed for guidance.

There was no visitation, no sudden apparition, but there was the slow renewal of strength. With it came the firm realisation that I would be able to meet whatever trials lay ahead of me.

I was in the little room for only 15 minutes, but the crisis had passed.

I opened the door and walked again to the bench, to the completion of the trial, to a future that I was sure would in time be free of my old fear.

Life Without Marriage

by ANITA COLBY

> Anita Colby, fashion and beauty consultant, is one of the millions of girls in the army of the unmarried. She knows that single girls need not be embittered old maids or frustrated career women and, from her own experience, tells how to achieve the happy life.

LET'S face the fact that there are thousands of women in any country who are never going to be married.

Some aren't even going to get the chance to say Yes or No!

Happily, the single state is no longer a matter of gloom, embarrassment or inferiority. Today, many girls *do say* 'no' to earnest proposals, rather than settle for a makeshift union. Who knows but that this courageous trend may help bring a new standard of respect and quality to marriage? We've seen too many broken homes and unions, most certainly not made in heaven.

People have asked me more often why I've never married than about any other phase of my personal or professional life.

The truth is I really don't know.

It's possible the right man hasn't come along as yet.

It's possible I've always been too engrossed in my work to recognise the right man if he has come along.

Maybe I've become too selective, too self-sufficient for my own good.

Perhaps I unconsciously think too much of my freedom and secretly fear the boredom that is always possible in more routine living.

I guess I've just never been fully and unequivocally in love. Lots of other women have this experience.

Truthfully, I still hope to marry some day because I'd like the permanent and complete companionship of the one-and-only man with whom I could share all of life. I still hope to have a home and children some day, too, for to me all of these things represent the most satisfying way of life.

If they never happen, however, I'll not press any panic buttons or scream for the smelling salts because my single life is and always has been a good and satisfactory one, and should be even better in the years ahead.

I certainly have no fear of the future as a single woman and no particular reluctance about facing it, if face it I must.

God has blessed me with a loving family—sister, mother and father—and an unusually happy home life. I have my work, a number of hobbies, and many activities in charitable organisations. These are the bulwarks against loneliness.

I'm not afraid of financial insecurity, either. I have made money, lost it, and gained confidence in the process.

The basic insecurity of the future concerns all of us, married and unmarried. Nothing in this life is certain anyhow. To be sure of a steady supply of life's necessities would siphon off much of the excitement life has always held for me.

Upon reading these last few statements, some woman is certain to say to me, "It's easy for you to talk. You had a modelling career, a movie career and a successful business career. Your life has been exciting. But I'm just a plain Jane. I have no beauty to attract men. You can be adjusted to spinsterhood, if you want, but I hate it and what it means."

Beauty attracts men, no doubt about it. But beauty is no passport to love. How do you account for the thousands of happy wives who are plain, even thoroughly unattractive? Others are downright ugly—even deformed. And hundreds of very pretty girls are single.

One can be beautiful, cultivate personality, have tenderness, understanding, zest, health and a lively well-informed mind—and still *not* find the mate that all of us long for, male and female alike.

Many women, who wholeheartedly lose themselves in the lives of others, find the answer to unmarried loneliness.

Who could not be inspired by Florence Nightingale? Beautiful, rich, intelligent, she left everything desirable to live in squalor and fight to establish the nursing profession. Certainly her story can give hope and a goal to any single girl.

If there is one secret to the successful single life for women, it is simply this: That it must be freely and definitely chosen as a means of greater service to humanity and the greater honour and glory of God!

The late Sister Elizabeth Kenny, one of the great unmarried of our time, stated the case succinctly and well.

"Just as enforced poverty," she said, "often brings out the worst in people, so does unwanted spinsterhood rouse bitterness and restless frustration in others. But there is supreme nobility in chosen poverty . . . freedom, dignity and fulfilment are possible in the single life only when dedication inspires it and solo living is a definite decision."

I am also inspired by Pope Pius XII's recent remark that it is the unmarried, *free of the detailed burdens and responsibilities of domesticity*, who have accounted for much of the progress of the human race and have been foremost among the builders and doers of all time.

"Vocation is God's call to a life especially consecrated to Him," the Pope continued. "It urges some girls to follow the religious life . . . others to sacrifice the happiness of marriage to lead a life more completely dedicated to good works *outside the religious life*."

Great doers among the unmarrieds include Clara Barton, founder of the Red Cross; Evangeline Booth, pioneer for the Salvation Army; Astronomer Maria Mitchell; Author

Emily Brontë; the remarkable Helen Keller; countless others.

Only a handful of years ago, as time is counted, could a woman own property herself, decide whom she'd wed or not wed, vote for the government of her country; until recently she was a native of a country but not a citizen.

Only since World War I have women been really free. Free financially, morally, physically, socially and professionally. Safe to go and come, to do or not do.

Women are the quiet doers by nature, those who can endure, the patient ones. We are noted for doing unpleasant work—over and over again. We are the housekeepers of the world, the comforters, the source of inspiration and encouragement, the binders of wounds, the steady watchers through feverish hours. We could face a frontier wilderness, or we could plan a masque ball. We can make a man live up to himself, make him wrest his dreams out of the impossible. We women can call for the best—and get it.

Not that there is any reason for women to be complacent today. We have equal rights, but what have we done with them? Is the government any better since women have had the vote? What about our schools, hospitals, prisons—the juvenile problems? Are these problems any better today because of us?

Around the corner from us is one of these crying needs. Perhaps, this is where you and I start.

I know that when God created me, He created me with a pattern and a purpose.

If I am attuned to the Lord, I will be shown my pattern and purpose, and in the fulfilling of that I will find the measure of serenity and power that I am supposed to possess.

Be Bold . . . *and mighty forces will come to your aid*

by ARTHUR GORDON

Don't be afraid to go out on a limb occasionally! Take a deep breath now and then and bite off more than you're sure you can chew! This writer tells you why you are stronger than you think. . . .

ONCE when I was facing a decision that involved (I thought) considerable risk, I took the problem to a friend much older and wiser than myself. "I'd go ahead," I said unhappily, "if I were *sure* I could swing it. But . . ."

He looked at me for a moment, then scribbled ten words on a piece of paper and pushed it across the desk. I picked it up and read, in a single sentence, the best advice I ever had: *Be bold—and mighty forces will come to your aid*.

It's amazing how even a fragment of truth will illuminate things. The words my friend had written were from a quotation, I discovered later, in a book by Basil King. They made me see clearly that in the past, whenever I had fallen short in almost any undertaking, it was seldom because I had tried and failed. It was because I had let fear of failure stop me from trying at all.

On the other hand, whenever I *had* plunged into deep water, impelled by a momentary flash of courage or just plain pushed by the rude hand of circumstance, I had always been able to swim until I got on the ground again.

Be bold—that was no exhortation to be reckless or foolhardy. Boldness meant a deliberate decision, from time to time, to bite off more than you were sure you could chew. But there was nothing vague or mysterious about the mighty forces referred to. They were the latent powers that all of us possess: energy, skill, sound judgment, creative ideas—yes, even physical strength and endurance in far greater measure than most of us realise.

Boldness, in other words, creates a state of emergency to which the organism will respond. I once heard a famous British mountaineer say that occasionally a climber will get himself into a position where he can't back down, he can only go up. He added that sometimes he put himself into such a spot on purpose. "When there's nowhere to go but up," he said, "you jolly well go up!"

The same principle works, less dramatically but just as surely, in something as commonplace as accepting the chairmanship of some civic committee, or even seeking a more responsible job. In either case, you know you'll have to deliver—or else. And unless you're hopelessly unqualified, you *will* deliver. Your pride, your competitive instinct, and your sense of obligation will see to it that you do.

These are some of the mighty forces that will come to your aid. They are, admittedly, psychic forces. But they are more important than physical ones. It was centrifugal force, in a hurtling pebble, that killed Goliath. But it was courage that enabled David to face the champion of the Philistines in the first place.

It's curious, actually, how spiritual laws often have their counterpart in the physical world. A college classmate of mine was a crack football player, noted particularly for his fierce tackling although he was much lighter than the average varsity player. Someone remarked that it was surprising that he didn't get hurt.

"Well," he said, "I think it goes back to something I discovered when I was a somewhat timid youngster playing sand-lot football. In one game, playing safety-man, I suddenly found myself confronting the opposing full-back, who had nothing but me between him and our goal-line. He looked absolutely gigantic! I was so frightened that I closed my eyes and hurled myself at him like a panicky bullet . . . and stopped him cold. Right there I learned that the harder you tackle a bigger player, the less likely you are to be hurt. The reason is simple: momentum equals weight times velocity."

In other words, if you are bold enough, even the laws of motion will come to your aid.

This personality trait—a willingness to put yourself in a position where you will have to extend yourself to the utmost—is not one that can be acquired overnight. But it can be taught to children and developed in adults. Confidence is a cumulative thing.

Boldness, of course, like any other virtue, can be pushed too far. Once, in my more impulsive days, I jumped out of an aeroplane just to see what it was like. I had a parachute, naturally—two, in fact—but I promptly wound up in a hospital with a broken ankle. I suppose I did achieve my main objective, which was to write a story about paratroopers with a certain amount of realism. But it was hardly worth it.

Still, for every time you thus overshoot your target, there are a hundred times that you undershoot it. In the famous Parable of the Talents, the servant who buries his master's money in the ground is reprimanded for failing to do anything with it or take any risk. And the servant's answer is significant. It could be summarised in three words: *I was afraid . . .*[1]

Fear, the opposite of boldness, is the most paralysing of all emotions. It can literally stiffen the muscles, as anyone knows who has ever been really scared. And (again the psychic-physical parallel holds) it can also stupefy the mind and the will. Most of us free-lance writers know this very well. When you are blessed—or cursed—with a vivid imagination, it's all too easy to become convinced that your energy is dwindling, that the flow of ideas is drying up, that your latest effort is also your last. Such thoughts are dangerous. Fears, like hopes and dreams, have a way of clothing themselves ultimately with reality. As Job said,

[1] *Matthew* 25. 25.

reviewing his troubles (and anticipating the psychiatrists by a couple of millennia), *The thing which I greatly feared is come upon me. . . .*[1]

Almost from the beginning of recorded history, mankind has recognised that the surest antidote for fear is religious faith. Belief—and trust—in a personal God makes a man bigger than himself and stronger than himself. Washington bore witness to this repeatedly; so did Lincoln. Joan of Arc was a shining example of the power of faith to transform an individual, and through an individual a whole nation.

This source of power is just as available to the rank and file as to the leaders. The man who believes firmly that the Creator of the universe loves him and cares infinitely what he does with his life—this man is automatically freed from much of the self-distrust that afflicts less certain men. Fear, guilt, hostility, anger—these are the emotions that stifle thought and impede action. By reducing or eliminating them, religious faith makes boldness possible, and boldness makes achievement possible.

Boldness is not always spectacular; there is also a quiet kind. I knew a city-dwelling family once that wanted to move to the country. They had no financial resources, but plenty of spiritual ones. Instead of counting the pennies and deciding the move was impossible, they calmly drew up a list of six requirements that they considered essential (actually, they agreed they would settle for five of the six). The place, they decided, would have to have a pleasant view, some shade trees, a stream or brook, some arable land to grow things, some pasture for animals, and it had to be near enough to the city for the father to milk the cows every morning and still commute to his job.

They finally found such a place, borrowed the money to make a down payment, and have been living there happily (and boldly, although no doubt the word would astonish them) ever since.

Job 3. 25.

This sort of self-confidence and decisiveness often marks a leader in the business world. The best executive I ever worked for was a man who made almost instantaneous decisions. "At least," he used to say wryly, "I make my mistakes quickly." On one occasion someone asked this man if he didn't believe in the old adage, "Look before you leap."

"No," he said cheerfully, "I don't." He thought for a minute, then added, "The trouble with that axiom is that if you look too long, or too often, you never leap at all."

A willingness to take chances, a solid faith in the ability of the individual to cope, God helping him, with just about any problem—these characteristics are part of the traditional American heritage. Is that spirit dying out? Some observers claim that our preoccupation with security is weakening it. Initiative, they say, is the instinctive response to lack. Security is the absence of lack. Can the two exist, side by side?

I think they can, simply because there are always new and more challenging worlds to conquer. We may be remembered as the generation that sought, and provided, material security for many. But we are also the generation that dared to pick the lock of the universe, the generation that invaded the heart of the atom. The risks were, and still are, appalling. But the mighty forces unleashed by our boldness will come to our aid some day in the form of unlimited light and heat and power for all mankind.

Love!

IF Helen Keller, blind and deaf, can find our world a thing of beauty, why is it that we with our full vision have such difficulty in seeing the loveliness about us? The answer, it would seem, is love. Or our lack of love.

What is love? How do we find it? To Miss Keller "love is not a vague and aimless sentiment, but a desire for good united with wisdom and fulfilled in work and deed." *God is love*, says John.

We think of love, of course, as that beautiful attraction of man for woman, of a mother for her child, but love goes beyond these familiar personal relationships. For one thing it can be the creative power that dissolves a poisonous hatred. It is the cohesive force that binds people together in understanding. Perhaps the greatest description of love is by Paul in 13 Corinthians:

Love suffereth long, and is kind; love envieth not; love vaunteth not itself, is not puffed up, doth not behave itself unseemly, seeketh not her own, is not easily provoked, thinketh no evil; rejoiceth not in iniquity, but rejoiceth in the truth; Beareth all things, believeth all things, hopeth all things, endureth all things.

                                    Norman Vincent Peale

My Luminous Universe
by HELEN KELLER

> Blind, deaf and speechless since the age of nineteen months, one of the world's most sensitive women writes of some of the lessons she has learned during her remarkable lifetime.

IT is difficult for me to answer when I am asked what are the main lessons life has taught me. Looking deeply into my inner self, I feel that ultimately I have not been influenced by any particular 'lessons', but rather by forces working on my subconsciousness that have borne me on an unseen current.

The tendencies which my teacher[1] divined and developed were the making of the ship that has carried me far out into the ocean of public life. Joy in adventure, travel and love of service to my fellow men were stronger than physical handicaps.

Instinctively I found my greatest satisfaction in working with men and women everywhere who ask not, "Shall I labour among Christians or Jews or Buddhists" but say rather, "God, in Thy wisdom help me to decrease the sorrows of Thy children and increase their advantages and joys." Blindness and deafness were simply the banks that guided the course of my life-ship until the stream joined the sea.

But there is one lesson I have consciously learned—that, although in Ecclesiastes it is said *There is no new thing under the sun*,[2] yet history is full of new meanings in every age and nation, which continually blossom and bear fruit. To my surprise I discovered in my Greek sayings,

[1] Anne Sullivan, who began teaching Helen Keller at the age of seven.
[2] *Eccl.* 1.9.

"There is no force so mighty in the world as perseverance." It never occurred to the writer of that rich sentence in ancient times that it would sow new seeds of significance until a day would come when the blind, the deaf, and the crippled would rise up in the might of purpose, compel their obstacles aside, and press onward to creative accomplishment.

I have caught rays of light from different thinkers—Socrates, Plato, Bacon, Kant, and Emanuel Swedenborg, the Swedish seer. With Socrates I believe in thinking out the meaning of words before committing them to speech. Plato's theory of the Absolute strengthens me because it gives truth to what I know is true, beauty to the beautiful, music to what I cannot hear, and light to what I cannot see. Swedenborg has shaken down the barriers of time and space in my life and supplied me with likenesses or correspondences between the world within and the world without, which give me courage and imagination beyond my three senses.

Thus I move from one philosophy to another, constructing out of a fragmentary outward environment a luminous, resonant universe.

These varied thoughts convince me that, blind or seeing, one is not happy unless one's heart is filled with the sun which never dissolves into gloom. God is that sun, and if one's faith in Him is not strong, He will somehow or other reveal one's powers and brighten the darkest days with His divine beams.

Since my seventeenth year I have tried to live according to the teachings of Emanuel Swedenborg. By 'church' he did not mean an ecclesiastical organisation, but a spiritual fellowship of thoughtful men and women who spend their lives for a service to mankind which outlasts them. He called it a civilisation that was to be born of a healthy, universal religion—good will, mutual understanding, service from all to each and each to all, regardless of dogma or ritual.

Swedenborg's religious works are in many long volumes, but their sum and substance are in three main ideas—God as Divine Love, God as Divine Wisdom, and God as Power for use. These ideas come as waves from an ocean which floods every bay and harbour of life with new potency of will, of faith, of effort.

By love I do not mean a vague, aimless sentiment, but a desire for good united with wisdom and fulfilled in work and deed. Because God is infinite, He puts resources into each human being that outrun the possibilities of evil. He is always creating in us new forms of self-development and channels through which, even if unaware, we may quicken new impulses towards civilisation, art, or humanitarianism.

My confidence in the final triumph of idealism over materialism does not spring from closing my mental eyes to the suffering or the evil-doing of men, but rather from a steadfast belief that good will climbs upward in human nature while the meanness and hatred drop into their native nothingness, and life goes on with unabated vigour to its new earth and heaven.

There are two ways to look at destiny, one from below and the other from above. In one view we are being pushed by irresistible forces, obsessed by the fear that war, ignorance, poverty, and barbarism will never be abolished. But looking up to the clock of Truth, I see that man has been civilised only a few minutes, and I rest in the assurance that out of the problems and tensions which disturb thinking minds and warm hearts there shall break the morning star of universal peace.

I have never let myself be bothered by the idea of a supernatural heaven, but I have a joyous sense of personal immortality. Life in the other world is just as real and full of change and wonder as on earth, but one is given eyes and ears to perceive far more clearly the varieties of good and constructive thought which the flesh conceals on earth.

In a sense souls transmigrate, not from place to place,

but through endless phases of personality. Angels and demons are all from the human race, and each chooses his dwelling either in the light or in the shadows. All peoples and kindreds who believe in God, yes, even those who worship idols from a desire to do good, are taught new concepts of Him and how to live for the peace and happiness of those around them.

Love and brotherhood and harmonious thoughts send fragrance and music into the atmosphere as they are wrought into service. Life in heaven is free from the clogs of time and the burdens of weight.

I do not believe that anyone ever attains perfection because that attribute belongs to the Infinite alone. But the longing for perfection, which is one way of loving God, causes one to grow nobler and to taste innumerable delights through eternity.

As I look to the future, I feel the thrill of challenge to greater self-realisation. I do not know what I shall do in the coming years, but I shall continue whatever services I can to the blind and others who are handicapped, and I intend to enlarge the studies which delighted me when I was young—philosophy and languages and the laws of the spirit.

I want to survey quietly the treasures of thought which I have gathered, but have not had leisure to explore. I do not know what they will lead me to, but I shall endeavour to gain fresh insights from my odyssey of work for the blind and the deaf. While I pursue my studies, I shall be sure that creative personalities will put a richer interpretation on my concepts of earth-life and fortify mankind for still higher areas of accomplishment.

No One Is Alone

by LORETTA YOUNG

> *"Last year I died," Dick Williams said. And he meant it, too. A beloved actress tells this unusual story of death, rebirth, and the importance of love.*

EVERY once in a while when you greet a friend casually, and expect a conventional reply, you catch the truth instead.

It happened to me recently when I recognised on my motion picture set a man I hadn't seen for a long time.

I said, "We've missed seeing you around. How've you been?"

"Well, I'm fine now," he replied; then after a moment's hesitation he blurted out, "but last year I died."

Dick Williams meant to be believed. "You may think it's a fantastic story," he said, "but I can prove every word of it."

Up to a point it wasn't fantastic at all. If anything, too heartbreakingly usual. What had once been simply an enthusiastic taste for strong drink became an obsession with Dick. He also had a malicious contempt for anyone with a dark skin. Frankly, he admitted he had done nothing to curb his intemperance nor his intolerance until, at last, as he put it: "My life deteriorated into common drunkenness. My wife left me. No dough. No job. And I was running out of friends . . . the way you do."

One couple who stuck by him, who realised how grim things had become, offered him their house as shelter while they were away on vacation. It was in that house that Dick 'died'.

When his friends returned, they found him cold on the floor, and a physician made the official pronouncement.

Dick had caught pneumonia there alone; his head too fuzzy, his body too weak, even to know it. So that seemed to be the end of his life story.

But at the mortuary a new undertaker was entrusted with the job of preparing him for a poor man's funeral. Dick laughed. "Lucky for me he was a beginner. When it came to the embalming fluid, he got scared and went to get a more experienced man to watch him. When they came back, my eyes were moving."

His next stop was the 'dead room' of a large hospital, the place where hopeless cases awaited the end. But once again the end didn't come.

The doctors, convinced now that something might yet be done, decided on a complicated method of administering oxygen. They made a frantic search for three nurses to undertake the constant care. Among the already overburdened staff there simply were not three available for that steady vigil. Now, at the twelfth hour, it looked as though Dick Williams's luck was out.

It was the Motion Picture Relief Association that finally located the nurses and, said Dick, "It was those three women who not only saved, but renewed, my life."

His first conscious impression was of an ebony face bending close to his own. For fifty long hours those negro nurses worked tirelessly, patiently, lovingly, to give him back his life. And, in the end, Dick said, "If they were out of my sight, I felt lost, insecure. I cried for them.

"In my rebirth I didn't just learn tolerance. I learned real, honest, brotherly love."

Dick found a job, a very humble job, when he was well enough. He had an objective. He wanted to buy each of those women a watch, the fancy kind with second hands and things that nurses dote on. Today they have their watches but, said Dick, "I doubt if they'll ever know what they *really* did for me."

The glow of light that lingered with me was not beamed from the story of his remarkable physical recovery. It was, instead, the idea that love had set him free. Really free.

Suppose those nurses had done their work grudgingly? Or simply dutifully? Would that have wrought the 'miracle'? Somehow Dick Williams didn't think so . . . and neither do I.

Probably they felt they had done a small thing, something in the line of duty. Yet here their goodness was, like a shining pebble dropped in a big pond, sending forth ever widening ripples.

It made me realise that our acts must be measured *by how lovingly we do them*.

Recently I realised, much to my surprise, for I have been doing it unconsciously, that every night just before I go to sleep I repeat the same little prayer of my childhood, with my same childhood faith and trust. Me, a grown-up woman, a Hollywood actress, a mother, a wife, saying just before I closed my eyes, "And please, dear God, make me a good girl."

Momentarily I was upset. One reads so much of complexes these days that simplicity is regarded as suspect. Could I be trying, subconsciously, to escape the responsibility for carrying an adult burden in an adult world? So I checked with my mother.

"Mother," I asked, "is there any special prayer that you say every night before you go to sleep?"

My mother, a wise servant of God, serving Him so faithfully and well for so many years, thought a minute and then said, "Yes, there is. I say, 'Give me a happy death and please, dear God, make me a good girl.'"

In the simplicity of that prayer, in the childlike attitude of the heart, lie, I am convinced, some of our biggest answers.

How to Be a Lovable Person
by SMILEY BLANTON

> She was attractive, intelligent, and much sought after by men—but only for a date or two. This is one of several cases which a distinguished psychiatrist presents while discussing the quality of 'balanced love'.

"WHY don't people love me?" The question came from Jane Young, an attractive young woman in her thirties who came to me for counsel.

"My parents never wanted me—I was the fourth daughter and they wanted a boy," she told me. "I was always terribly conscious of their disappointment."

Jane's beauty has a cold quality. One could feel sorry for an unwanted childhood but not nearly as sorry as she felt for herself. As we talked, it was easy to detect a hard core of selfishness inside her. She had been sought after by men, but none had pursued her very long. One story she told was especially revealing, and it was interesting that she remembered it so well.

Jane and a young engineering teacher, who was very fond of her, went to a dance. It was a crisp, beautiful night, with the stars shining. Walking home, the young man, in a somewhat lyrical mood, stopped for a moment and recited a bit of poetry:

> ". . . Look, how the floor of heaven
> Is thick inlaid with patines of bright gold. . . .
> Such harmony is in immortal souls . . ."

Jane, even though in no mood for poetry, could have been sensitive enough to her friend's feelings to compliment him. Instead, she said stiffly: "Come on—we'll catch cold. We must be getting home." The young man did not remain her suitor long.

She blamed her troubles on her parents' lack of love and understanding. In some ways, she was right. Yet, at no time in her life had Jane grasped the simple idea that *the reason so many people who want love don't receive it is that they have never learned how to be lovable.*

Compare Jane to Betty, who is the same age, but not nearly as attractive. Betty's hours are spent drying her children's tears, cooking meals, baking cakes for a church social, sewing and mending. She has a ready smile for everyone—and a very special one for her athletic husband, who is devoted to her.

People can't help but love Betty because she thinks of the happiness of the people she loves—before her own.

Whether a person develops lovability depends very much upon the way he or she is brought up. Parents have need for great care in order to love wisely.

Walter Jordan's case points this up in quite a different way. The youngest of four boys, he was a sensitive, intelligent child. His mother became an invalid when he was about fourteen. Since the other brothers were all older and out in the world, much of the mother's care fell upon him. He never married. After work each day he would care for his mother—taking her out to dinner, reading to her, arranging for her to see friends, seeing that she got to church. When he was thirty-five, his mother died. He had become so used to the idolatrous affection which his mother gave him that he found life very depressing without it.

About a year later he married. Within two years he and his wife came to our Church Clinic because the marriage was on the rocks. The reason was obviously located in Walter's complete self-centredness. He wanted his meals just so; to eat at the restaurants of his choosing and attend the shows he picked. Dominating people so much, he had very few friends and his wife found life quite intolerable.

At the clinic the psychological reasons for his unattractive attitudes were revealed to him. He learned to understand the pathos of his mother's life and her well-meaning, but ill-advised, indulgence of him. His understanding became objective, he could see the reasonableness of other people's viewpoints and his own boorish actions became clear. Later a very rich spiritual experience came to him in the church. He became, in time, a thoughtful, unselfish and lovable personality.

Here was a man hurt by too much unwise love, while Jane's happiness was destroyed by lack of love. Yet children who are given a proper sense of relationship to God and their fellow man cannot be miserable adults. And many orphans and even abandoned youngsters become happy, lovable, balanced adults who radiate good will.

One of the most important ways to develop a balanced love in a youngster is to teach the child to love God. If one loves God, one cannot be selfish and unemotional.

Both children and adults shut out love when they build up barriers and suspicions between themselves and other people. If they make the attempt to know and love Christ, whose life and example they cannot criticise, in time they will find the good, or Christ, in other people which they can love. This spirit so captures them and irradiates their personalities that they become attractive and lovable to other people.

Dr. Smiley Blanton, M.D., is the author of *Love or Perish*, published by The World's Work (1913) Ltd.

Put Your Difficulties to Work

FRANCIS QUARLES, the English poet, once wrote: "He that has no cross will have no crown." This is a succinct description of what I consider to be one of the noblest of all themes in living—personal triumph over adversity.

I heard someone make the interesting observation that the worst affliction of life is never to be afflicted. This means that often the greatest value in life is most apparent and most treasured when some of it is denied. It also means that a human being who has not met trouble and fought it has not *really* lived. The person who engages in a struggle against obstacle or handicap—especially in a full-scale fight in which body, mind and spirit are put to work simultaneously—lives life to the very hilt because all his fibres and senses are drawn into play.

The world has always cherished the theme of David and Goliath. From childhood we thrill to the idea of 'The Little Engine That Could', of the underdog who turns the tables. Today, America is full of amazing stories showing how people have achieved remarkable victories against heavy odds.

In the following stories you will see that whether the Goliath be blindness or poverty or sickness, it is faith that brings about victory. The inspiring lesson to be learned is that people win their battles not only despite handicaps, but often *because* of them.

Norman Vincent Peale

Poverty Never Made Us Poor

by IVY BAKER PRIEST

> *What was the secret behind the wonderful sense of security this pioneer Mormon family possessed? Ivy Baker Priest, Treasurer of the United States, tells how early hardships were turned into advantages during her childhood.*

SHORTLY after I came to Washington, a friend asked me what was the most difficult problem I ever had to face. I found myself answering without thinking: "Poverty."

It seems odd to people that the Treasurer of the United States, who is concerned with billions of dollars, was once concerned with poverty. Time and again our family made plans for the future, then abandoned them because there wasn't enough money to carry the plans out.

My father worked in the copper fields. He would lease out a stake from one of the companies and work it himself. If he hit it right, times were good.

But if anything went wrong, times could be bad indeed.

Mother had plans that were abandoned, too. Her dreams were for her family. She had seven children—I was the eldest—and felt strongly that each of us should have a normal home life, yet every time she was about to reach her goal, some new disaster entered her life.

From the first, we had to get used to this feast-or-famine existence in my family. Once, when we were in a feast time, my father and mother moved into a large house in Bingham Canyon, Utah. It was just a frame building, set on a hill along with a row of other mining-town houses, close up to a narrow street, and yet even Mother's home was not really hers for long.

One day there was another accident at the mine. My

father's leg was broken, and he was out of work for months. We very shortly ran out of money. Mother turned to our church's welfare programme for aid. She also turned the home she was so proud of into a boarding house.

Then, in addition to 50 children romping around outside, seven children of her own, an injured husband to care for, there were 30 miners to feed three times a day.

Even such things as family prayers, for instance, were far from normal in my childhood. Prayers had an unusual function in our home. With most families mealtime is a family time. Mealtime in our house was just the opposite because we all had to work getting food ready for the men.

Mother—I don't remember much about when she ate. After everyone else was served, I suppose. But at any rate mealtime was not a family time in our home. So we grew to depend on family prayers as a time to be together in the presence of God. "You can face adversity much better when you don't feel you're alone," my father used to say.

My mother and father were Mormons. The fact that they were Mormons was responsible for their meeting in the first place. There is a practice in the Mormon Church for young men to devote two years of their lives in missionary work. My father went to England during his two missionary years and there met Mother, who was a member of the Mormon Church in England. They fell in love. On his return to America he worked and saved to pay Mother's passage to the States. They married and moved to Utah.

We have a belief in the Mormon Church that we call 'eternal progression'. We believe in a stage of existence before birth, as well as after death. We believe that man progresses from one stage in his existence to another; and I was taught by my family that while we are in the stage known as 'life', each of us is given a separate set of talents.

Our objective in life is to use these talents to the utmost, wherever they lead us.

This is the kind of objective my mother and father had.

"If we don't use our talents, that is where we fail," my mother used to say, out in the kitchen, whenever one of her own best-laid plans went *a-gley*. "We must try to make sound plans. But we should never set our heart on one goal so firmly that our world will come tumbling down around our feet if we can't reach it. How do we know what path God has in mind for our talents?"

I have found this very helpful all my life.

When I was a young girl, I decided I would like to become a lawyer. I actually did get as far as entering the University of Utah. Then one snowy day in 1928, when he was still a vigorous man, my father was run over by a car. His skull was fractured. He never recovered. He lay ill for the last six years of his life, and his income stopped completely. There was no choice but for me to go to work.

"Don't worry," Mother said. "Education is not a separate and complete experience. It is a preparation for the experience of living."

I never did get back to college. I went to work immediately as a telephone operator. The younger children took whatever jobs they could find such as caddying and selling newspapers. But when we pooled our incomes, there still wasn't always enough to go around.

It was at times like this, all through my childhood, that one of the very finest of the Mormon practices came to our aid: our welfare programme. We tithe our income in the Mormon Church. Part of our tithe goes to what we call the Lord's Storehouse, modelled after the Lord's Storehouse in the Old Testament, where people in trouble could come for aid. I don't know how we'd have made out without the storehouse. But one of the most beautiful parts of this Mormon programme is that we were always expected to contribute to the storehouse, even while receiving.

We contributed time, instead of goods. The children

could go down to the storehouse workrooms. My mother could go down, too, and sew or help in the cannery. It kept us from feeling we were charity cases, which we weren't. Even accepting aid was a part of our religious life.

In 1934, my father passed into the last stage of his own 'eternal progression', and just four years ago my mother joined him. But they had used their talents to the utmost.

My father, for instance, contributed his gift for careful, prayerful judgment and his innate wisdom both to his family and to literally hundreds of miners who might never have known such a man if my father had become a judge.

My mother contributed her cheerfulness, her astounding ability to accept her lot, roll up her sleeves and start again.

All their lives my mother and father had a security that was astounding under the circumstances of their lives. They knew they could depend on their storehouse. That storehouse took away the fear of not having enough to eat. But even more important they had a spiritual storehouse within themselves that they contributed to always.

A security like theirs cannot be wrecked by adversity, because insecurity comes from fear of having to abandon one's plans. My mother and my father never, really, had to abandon their plans.

That's how it was that, although poverty was the worst problem our family had to face, not one of the seven children ever lacked the sense of being entirely secure. Which, I guess, is as fine a tribute as anyone could ever pay to his parents.

My Favourite Thanksgiving Story
by DOUGLAS MacARTHUR

> *This is the story of a Thanksgiving dinner given in a small home in Midwest America over thirty years ago. It might easily never have happened at all; yet it may affect the future of the Orient. That is why it is General MacArthur's favourite Thangsgiving story.*

IN 1908 Hachiro Yuasa, a 17-year-old Japanese boy, said good-bye to his parents and sailed for the United States. Raised in an earnest Japanese Christian family, Hachiro had long dreamed of coming to America to live the simple, Christian life of an American farmer and, later, to get his university education.

On ship, thin, young Hachiro composed an imaginary letter telling of his long-awaited arrival in California. He pictured his father at dinner, holding the letter, as he bowed his head for grace:

"Our Heavenly Father, we come together again, as a family. Yet one of us is away. May Hachiro's presence be with us through his warm letter to us. In Christ's name . . ."

But Hachiro didn't write that letter—not for eleven years. His words about America always seemed to come out bitter. He did not find the Christianity he expected. In the restaurants no one said grace. Once, at a Y.M.C.A., he laid his pocket change on a dresser in the men's dorm before going out to look for a job. When he returned, the 'Y' secretary gave him a stern lecture about the care of money.

"But why?" Hachiro wanted to know. "Isn't this the Young Men's *Christian* Association?"

And where was this respect for individuals? California

in 1908 was not an easy place for an Oriental to live. Prejudice ran high. In time, Hachiro did find work picking cherries in the fruit fields near San Jose; but his hours were from sun-up to sun-down and, at irrigation time, far into the night. Evenings, when he wasn't working in the fruit fields, he would wash dishes in the farm kitchen. There, he attacked the pots and greasy water that were to become such a part of his life.

Standing over the sink full of dirty dishes and some of his own tears, he again composed in his mind a letter about America. But again he did not write it, because it would be bitter:

"I am not a brother to Americans. Our working crew is Japanese. Only the foreman is American. He spoke to me once. He said: 'See? Them too green. No pick 'em.'

"But I feel better now. I have formed a layer of ice around my heart which protects me."

After two years of farm labour during the day and dirty dishes at night, Hachiro realised he was not making the headway in English he would need to enroll in an American university. So, in 1910, still thin and frail, Hachiro Yuasa moved to Oakland and went for a few months each to grade school, then high school.

He supported himself by house cleaning, window washing, and lawn mowing, at 25 cents an hour. He was a silent young man, moving solemnly about his chores. Hachiro liked the mechanical work—he didn't have to talk to anyone and it gave him a chance to practise his verbs.

"I am cutting the lawn, you are cutting the lawn . . . I mow, you mow, he mows. We mow the lawn . . .'

At the end of four years in this country, Hachiro, thinner than ever, had put aside seven $10 gold pieces and learned enough English to be accepted as a freshman at Kansas State. He had reached his goal, but he wasn't ready, even yet, to let the ice melt from his heart.

Eleven years passed.

While Yuasa was doing graduate work in Urbana,

Illinois, the Reverend and Mrs. Roger Augustine of that town decided to share their Thanksgiving with a foreign student. Hachiro was invited.

Hiding behind a shell of scholarly and scientific reserve, Hachiro arrived at the modest home. But at the door he was greeted by a real smile, and Mr. Augustine took Hachiro's hand in both of his.

Hachiro smiled back reluctantly, on his guard.

Dinner was ready. He sat down at the table with the family of four: mother, father, and two children. Behind a set smile, Hachiro was watching closely for the first sign that they might be fooling . . . Perhaps they really wanted him to do the dishes.

Then, carving knife in hand, the father bowed his head.

"Our Father: We have come together strangers. Let us part forever friends."

They meant him! Struggle as he might against it, memories came flooding back of Hachiro's own family. Grace before meals. The warm, close-knit family circle. He looked at the faces around him. There could be no doubt about it: these people liked him, wanted to know him, thought of him not as an Oriental, but as a person. An individual.

That night Hachiro wrote to his mother the letter about America he had put off for so many years.

"I was wrong when I looked for a whole government or a job or a school to respect me as an individual," he wrote. "This is not where to find Christianity. Love and kindliness are things that happen inside each man. The individual the person-to-person relationship—*that* is the thing."

Hachiro soon began to find friends. He told one of his instructors about a research problem that had been bothering him. The professor said, "Drop up to my house tonight, and we'll go over it. I'm glad you asked me. I've been interested in your work."

He told a fellow graduate student he hadn't made many

friends. "We'd like to have you in our science fraternity," said the young man. "But you always seemed so busy."

When Hachiro completed his work at the university, he had a new goal firmly rooted in his mind: show Japan the importance of the individual being.

Hachiro returned to the Orient in 1924 and took a post as professor of entomology at Kyoto Imperial University, the centre of Japan's scholastic life. But while his reputation as scientist and teacher quickly soared, his own dissatisfaction with the kind of education offered at Kyoto grew, too.

The formal, stereotyped schools in Japan offered no chance for the personal relationships that Yuasa had found all-important. There was no discussion, no questioning of what was spoken from the lectern. Student and teacher were separated by an impassable gulf of formality.

Finally, Yuasa could stand it no longer. He spoke out against god-shelves in school rooms, the bowing to Imperial Portraits. He took a stand for Christian principles. Young students, feverish over Japan's successes in China, reported him to their military instructors. Hachiro began to see his name chalked on the walls:

"Down with the traitor Yuasa!"

Forced to resign, Yuasa left Japan for America. Many of his friends think it was just in time. During the years of World War II that followed, it seemed to Dr. Yuasa that his life was a failure. . . .

Five months after the bomb was dropped on Hiroshima Dr. John MacLean, minister of a large church in Virginia, got up and made a suggestion that the United States, by some act of love, show the world a Christianity more powerful than war. His idea spread, and the 'act of love' soon focused on a new kind of University for Japan, the International Christian University. Plans were drawn up.

The school would be for students of all faiths, an experiment in stressing the importance of the individual in contrast to the dictatorship teachings of pre-war Japan.

Living-rooms in faculty apartments, for instance, would be oversized to encourage informal discussion groups right in the professor's homes. On school property was planned a co-operative farm. Allowing professors to pitch in and work with their hands beside the students would develop a new kind of relation to authority.

The proposed University had the backing of more American churches than had ever before co-operated on a single project. Help came, too, from labour and from management; from pacifist Quakers and from military men; from liberals and from conservatives.

In Japan, meanwhile, the response to the idea of this new school was amazing. Out of a crippled economy, Japanese people in 1949 raised over 160 million yen (about $45,000) for the building fund, 95% of the money coming from non-Christians.

When International Christian University opened its doors in April, 1952, the man chosen as President of this great university experiment—a man who learned about individual freedom at the grass roots level in America—was Hachiro Yuasa.

Seeing-Eye People

by CAROLE URICH

> *A courageous minister and his wife win a permanent place in the hearts of their congregation by proving that even though they are both blind, eyes aren't essential to do God's Work.*

IN March 1951, my husband, John Urich, was summoned to Grace and St. Paul's Lutheran Church in New York City on a six months' trial basis. Not many ministers go through a trial period before they are called. But it was different for John and me.

We are both blind. So we were really on trial!

Before we faced the challenge, we looked at the whole situation as we always do when we have to make a turn in the road. Now, how can sightless people *look* at anything? I'll tell you how: For the blind, or the seeing, there is always an inner light, if they want to look for it. It's the luminous hand of God pointing the way.

Anyway, John and I looked at the whole situation.

"No congregation is going to call a blind pastor just because he is able to make it to and from the pulpit on Sunday morning," John said. "We have work to do."

We got busy at once. John organised a Church Cabinet of people representing all the varied activities of the congregation. It gave a focus and a sense of direction to everything the church did. John began by perking up the teenage group and the young adults, and I organised a young girls' choir, began playing piano for the kindergarten, and organ for Sunday School.

John and I met at Kansas State School for the Blind, were married when John was a senior and I a junior at the University of Kansas. There wasn't enough money for both of us to attend school. I knew I could cook and iron without that B.A., so I settled for the MRS. degree. I earned some extra money ironing shirts. John and I earned a bit more singing and playing our songs at club meetings and churches. We learned early not to worry. We knew God was on our side.

After John graduated from the University, we went to Washington where he got a job as a dictaphone operator. He worked at it for four years, and his work was always so perfect no one ever had to do any erasing. One day John told his pastor of his secret desire to be a minister. Dr. Oscar Blackwelder hesitated for less than a second and said:

"John, I know you can."

A year later my husband entered the Lutheran Theological Seminary at Philadelphia. Because there were no textbooks in Braille at the Seminary, John collected volunteers to read the regular textbooks to him. Often they studied long into the night, and I'd make the coffee for them. At graduation in 1950, John was eighth in the entire student body.

For nine months after graduation John was a substitute for pastors who were ill. He did very well, but everyone was doubtful about a blind minister. Then John was given his six months' trial . . .

Grace and St. Paul's is an old church, one of the oldest in New York. Though it has four hundred members, only one third of them live in Manhattan. The rest are still loyal members, but they've moved to outlying sections of the city, and across the river into New Jersey.

John began visiting them, when they were in need, whether he was summoned or not. Bonnie, our seeing-eye dog, always goes with him. They travel by subway, bus and ferry to reach his scattered flock.

We have a four-room apartment. I cook, clean, and do some of the laundry, determined that our apartment be more than just neat. People who visited us would be quick to overlook dirt, but that was all the more reason to have everything spotless. So I learned to spend patient hours on my knees with cleansing brush, scrubbing out every corner.

John carefully rehearsed all phases of his church service. Handling Communion, for example, loomed as a very difficult problem since he would have to serve the wine cups and bread on a precision basis. Then, thank God, one of the congregation came up with an idea. Inside the Communion rail, a cord was tacked to the floor, pegs placed on the cord in the exact positions where members of the congregation would be kneeling. By moving his foot along the cord and touching the pegs, John knew exactly where to stop! On his first Communion Sunday John didn't spill a drop!

Soon teenagers and young adults started to invite us to

their events. Sometimes it would be a dinner or a play, or baseball, which is John's first love in sports. He's a Giant fan.

For three mornings a week, John was supplied a secretary who reads the mail, and then John answers it. She fills out the certificates for weddings, baptisms, and funerals, and John arranges his schedule for them.

Finally, the six months' trial period was up, and Hans Classen, president of our church, called John to a general meeting. I shall never forget that night.

Hans Classen stood up and his voice rang clear and certain across the crowded room. "John Urich, we are proud to call you as our permanent pastor."

If the congregation had any doubts during the trial period, they were gone. They knew that John needed no seeing-eye dog to lead them in God's way.

Ordeal By Water

by MARILYN BELL

WITH COMMENT BY GUS RYDER

The 16-year-old Canadian girl who conquered Lake Ontario, reveals here the technique she used for reaching a goal which had heretofore eluded all who sought it.

IT was raining pitchforks. There was a flash of lightning, and I saw rain sweep across the pier in waves. Then the night was black again, except for spotlights that lit up the United States Coast Guard hut where the great distance-swimmer Florence Chadwick was waiting for the storm to let up. Miss Chadwick was going to try swimming from Youngstown, New York, across Lake Ontario, to Toronto, Canada. I was going to try the swim, too. Little Pete Willinsky, whose father owned the small, 16-foot boat that was to pilot me from New York to Canada, huddled close and looked out over the lake.

"I bet those waves are big as a house," he said.

"What time is it?" I asked my trainer, Gus Ryder.

Gus said it was already past the time for the swim to start; it was 11.00 p.m.

Even while he was speaking, there was a little clapping from the crowd. Miss Chadwick came out and looked up into the rain. She tucked her hair into her cap; then she went quickly down to the black water and slipped in. There was another clapping at the sight of her long, beautiful strokes, 80 to the minute. I said to myself, "Holy cow! If she keeps that up, I'll never catch her." Shortly, I plunged in, too.

(Editor's note: Italics indicate the comments of Marilyn's coach, Gus Ryder.)

An hour out, Chadwick slowed down. She began to pace herself, and Marilyn passed her.

Marilyn's own team was strung out in a column in front of her. I was nearest, in a lifeboat. With me were 13-year-old Pete Willinsky; Jack Russell, who manned the lifeboat; and a reporter from the Toronto Star. Lightning flashes lit the pilot yacht up ahead. In it were Marilyn's parents; a doctor; more reporters, with two-way radios; and some observers.

And behind us, out in the water, came little Marilyn.

She seemed just a child. She was so small, all alone there in the blackness, only 16 years old, dreading the night and the cold and the eels. She hated the eels. "If I feel an eel," she had said, "I'll scream."

The reporters' voice startled me: "Still think she can make it?"

I looked at him and smiled. I knew he was remembering the statement I'd made to the press before the swim: that Marilyn could outlast Chadwick and would conquer the tricky currents and winds, the cold, the sheer size of the lake. From Youngstown, New York, to Toronto is 32 miles.

The English Channel swim is only 22 miles. "Let's wait and see," I said.

About 2.00 a.m., I think it was, I looked up from the water. It had stopped raining, but there were no stars. To the west, and behind me, I could see the tiny green light of Florence Chadwick's boat. For a moment I thought it had stopped. Ahead I could see the light from Gus's boat. But it seemed far away, and I suddenly felt alone and sort of sorry for myself. Gus had warned me about this.

"It isn't the lake; it's your own mind that will be your real enemy," he had said.

I looked at my watch. It was after four. Marilyn had been swimming in waves that were over my head for more than five hours. The reporter came over to me. "I think maybe Chadwick's boat has stopped," he said. Then, while we were talking, word came over the radio confirming that Florence Chadwick was in trouble. She was sick, exhausted. She had been pulled out.

I wondered whether to tell Marilyn right away. I remembered, before we started, I had taken her aside and whispered, "I want you to kneel down and ask God to guide you. We'll do the same on the boat."

Now, the memory of how she prayed reassured me, and I decided not to say anything about Chadwick yet. Later, when she needed encouragement, I thought.

Just before dawn I felt the first eel. It was slimy and it slid along my leg and its little suction-cup mouth latched on to my leg just where my bathing suit stopped. I knew he would stick there until he had sucked his fill of blood unless I got rid of him. For a minute I thought I was going to panic.

Then, for some strange reason, a scene popped into my mind. It was just before the swim, and my music teacher at school had taken me aside and said, "Now when you're out there alone on the lake, don't pray to make the shore, just pray to swim for one more hour."

I said aloud to the eel, "Well, I can't swim for one more

75

hour with you latched to me," and with loathing, I reached down and squeezed his mouth until the suction broke, and I flung him away from me and started swimming very fast until I felt I was away from him.

By early morning all of Canada knew who Marilyn Bell was. Broadcasts told how she was 16, weighed 119 pounds, was blonde, stood only 5 ft. 2 in. high, went to high school and sang in the choir at the United Church on Sundays. They told how she had already beaten Chadwick, but they said that she was tiring.

It was true; Marilyn was tiring. I counted her strokes. Down to 50 a minute. But she had a right to be tired. She had been swimming for eight hours.

For a little while after I learned that Florence Chadwick had given up, I felt stronger. I looked up and I could see Toronto in the distance. For the first time I began to believe I might make the shore.

But I was so sleepy. And Pete Willinsky didn't help. Poor little Pete. He was at the rail of the lifeboat, looking at me, and I watched his eyelids close slowly. I had to laugh. But it made me sleepy, too. Pete woke himself up and called out:

"Go! Go! Go! Marilyn!"

And then he went back to sleep. Poor Pete . . .

At four in the afternoon—Marilyn had been swimming for 17 hours—I drew close and saw that she was crying.

I checked with the doctor. He talked things over briefly with Marilyn's parents and left it up to me whether or not to take her out. "Let's go on a while longer," I said.

At five in the afternoon I hit another low ebb. I began swimming mechanically. I didn't really know what I was doing. Gus held up a sign: "Remember Canada!" That helped, for a while. Then I grew exhausted again.

At dusk, all of Canada knew that Marilyn had only four miles to go. Radio broadcasts and newspaper headlines were carrying her story, hourly, then every half-hour, then stroke by stroke.

Canada began to come to the waterside.

Thousands arrived. Then tens of thousands. Three hundred thousand, waiting. Waiting. They sensed that, by the grace of God, she just might make it.

For a while I was sure I would have to quit. I couldn't feel anything from the waist down. Then suddenly I looked up and saw my best friend, Joan Cooke. Gus had brought her out from Toronto. She swam beside me for a while, and I seemed to take strength from her.

I looked closely at Marilyn. She didn't look well. She had only two miles to go. I told her that if she finished, the Canadian National Exhibition had decided to give her $7,500 of Chadwick's prize money. I could tell by the way Marilyn responded that she didn't really grasp what I said.

"Marilyn! Marilyn!" I called. And I held up a sign.

I opened my eyes. And I realised that I had been swimming, unconscious. I just had to stop.

"Marilyn!" I called again.

From the distance I heard Gus again, and I looked up and saw his sign: "For the crippled kids!"

Poor Gus. Poor kids at the pool. Gus and I teach crippled children to swim. I put my head down and started out again. I wasn't praying for an hour; I was praying for just 15 minutes. I said over and over to myself . . . If you stop . . . one more time . . . you . . . will . . . never . . . never . . . start . . . again. . . .

Marilyn wasn't swimming in a straight line now. She was responding to my calls as if she were a robot. There was a strange silence that settled around the boat as we drew closer to the breakwater. There were hundreds of small craft circling about. From our boat we could now see clearly the thousands of people on the shore.

Marilyn was almost to the breakwater. She was swimming jerkily, automatically. Now we could hear the conversations of the people as they crowded down.

Then rockets began to burst, and a great cheer broke like thunder from the shore, Marilyn touched the breakwater.

Our Different Gifts

by PAUL ANDERSON

> "Too weak to live," doctors once concluded about Paul Anderson as a boy. Yet this 'weakling' is now called "the strongest man in the world". Here's how it happened.

It seemed strange that I, Paul Anderson from Toccoa, Georgia, should be lying in a hotel bed in Moscow and looking out of the window into a peaceful June sky. Our team of six weightlifters was scheduled to compete with Russia's best athletes the next morning at Gorky Park in Moscow.

I wanted to get to sleep, but it wasn't easy. The ornate design of the wall paper above my head was unreal. So was my being here, thousands of miles from home. I thought of my most enthusiastic rooter—my mother—who had been so excited about this trip. Perhaps she was now comparing my present situation to the time years ago when doctors thought I was too weak to live.

That was when I was seven years old. I would come home from school tired and cross. I was losing weight. One day when I awoke shivering and feverish, Mother called the doctor.

I was taken to the hospital, where there were more doctors, more examinations. Outside the bedroom, I could hear hushed voices. The words "Bright's disease" and "attacks the kidneys" drifted in to me. When the doctors left, Mother come in. And I sensed from the worried look on her face that I was quite ill.

While the doctors were doing all they could, Mother took up her vigil. Whenever I fell asleep, she went to the phone and called all the clergymen she knew and asked for prayers. She called her friends, too. "Paul is dying," she said. "We need your special help."

And then she waited. For five days I hovered between life and death.

The doctors expected me to slip quietly downhill. Then the time for the crisis passed and nothing happened. Mother left to call the churches again. "If Paul can stick it out," she said, "it will be because of our prayers."

I was better on the sixth day. I remember waking up and finding Mother at my bedside. "You're over the worst part. I'm sure of it. Now we can get you on your feet again."

It wasn't easy. Bright's disease leaves you weak and thin. Some people never really recover.

"A lot of people prayed for you," my father told me when I returned home. "You can't let them down. You've got to get strong again."

Slowly my parents coached me along, encouraged me to eat and exercise, play rugged sports. Their campaign was so successful that by the time I got to high school I weighed 185 pounds and played football.

When I entered Furman University on scholarship, I weighed over 200 pounds—quite a contrast to the frail 60-pound boy who left the hospital just ten years earlier.

Home for summer vacation after my first year at college I decided to work with weights to build up my legs for football. I quickly became fascinated with this sport.

My family helped me to rig up a home gym. We didn't buy any professional equipment, but used what we could find around town. I still use homemade equipment. My favourite weight is 'The Thing', two thrasher wheels attached to a bar. It weighs over 800 pounds. I use it for deep knee bends to develop my legs and shoulders.

As I became more interested in the ancient sport of weightlifting, I learned more about its terms and contest rules. In a weightlifting meet you are expected to make three different kinds of lifts. In the *clean* and *jerk* the weights are placed on the floor, first lifted shoulder high, and then with a quick stiffening of the legs, jerked above your head. More difficult is the *press*, where the weights are lifted from the floor to your shoulders, then pushed slowly above your head. The most difficult is called snatch where the weights are lifted above your head in one sweeping motion from the floor.

I entered national competitions, winning a number of events. Then in June 1955, the offer came from the Amateur Athletic Union to take the trip to Russia.

Weightlifting is a major sport in Russia, equivalent to baseball in the United States. It arouses a tremendous interest. I had the feeling that Russian sports fans would be looking for weakness in the Americans, hoping for it. Yet, if they were real sports fans, they could be influenced by a championship performance. Our American team had to be ambassadors of the best.

The night before the meet came, and I couldn't sleep. Too many thoughts. In Corinthians Paul talks about *the different gifts* God gave us.

With me it is a feeling of gratitude for my gift of strength. So I reminded myself that night in the Moscow hotel that I had a special obligation to use this gift for God and country.

Gorky Park is not a regular stadium. It is an open-air amphitheatre. As we prepared for the competition, the rain outside was coming down hard enough to have driven most audiences home. But that night there were more than 15,000 spectators.

Every seat was sold. Crowds were standing around at the backs and along the sides. A Russian band played the Star-Spangled Banner.

First there were the lighter class lifts, and in these the Russian and American competitors were pretty evenly matched. Then came the heavyweights.

The Russian heavyweight champion, Medrediev, stepped up, dried his hands, reached down to the bar in front of him. The crowd cheered as he snatched 298 pounds, pressed 325 pounds, did 370 pounds in the clean and jerk.

Then it was my turn.

In the snatch I handled 316 pounds, in the press 404½ pounds, and 426 pounds in the clean and jerk. The Russian announcer spoke:

"Paul Anderson totals 1,146½ pounds. The American has just set two new world records. Never have we seen such weights lifted."

None of this would have been possible but for the prayers of others. I'm convinced of that. Nor would I be alive today if I had been born of godless parents. Realising this after my victory in Moscow made me grateful all over again for my parents, my country and God.

Editor's Note: Since writing this article, Paul Anderson competed in the 1956 Olympics at Melbourne, Australia, winning the heavyweight weight-lifting gold medal for the United States.

Give Yourself Away

ONE of the greatest of all secrets of happiness is to know how to give yourself. Outgoingness is a chief quality of the well organised person. Save and hoard yourself and you will lose yourself. Give yourself and you will find yourself.

Following are stories of people the world over who are motivated by deep feelings of sacrifice and love. Some are important and others are little-known individuals, but all are people who are the centres of both great and small dramas. A New York advertising man thrillingly describes how individuals in everyday life have been discovering heroic opportunities to give and receive. A young suburban couple learn the value of tithing, and a Californian builds a flourishing food business on a principle of free meals.

Have you ever thought of how *you* could give *yourself* away?

Norman Vincent Peale

What Is Tithing?

by JOHN and ELIZABETH SHERRILL

> *Can you go broke giving away ten per cent of your income? This is the personal experience of two young people who find the true meaning behind one of the oldest religious practices of all times.*

WHEN we saw the tramp coming towards us we felt a little embarrassed. He had a withered arm and a week's growth of beard. We fixed our eyes on the sidewalk beyond him and walked a little faster. But our jovial and elderly companion walked right up to the chap. "A hot lunch?" we heard him say. "How much would that cost you?"

"A bowl of soup—twenty cents, mister. Add a sandwich and it's fifty cents."

"All right, I'll make you a bargain. Here's a dollar. Buy your meal, but do something for me, will you? Give ten cents of this away to somebody else."

"What was that all about?" we asked. "You don't really think he'll keep that bargain?"

"Perhaps not," our friend said. "But if he does, it could change his life. I know. I'm a tither."

Tithing, we remembered, means giving ten per cent of your income to charity. As so often happens when an unusual idea is called to our attention, we began to see the word everywhere. For instance, an Associated Press article told of a group of farmers in Abernathy, Texas, who had pledged one tenth of their crop to the church. Each man reported a bumper harvest, more than enough to make up for what he gave away. Albert Hart, who had dedicated five of his 50 acres, reported that cotton on his tithed land grew a foot higher than on the rest of the land.

The farmers explained these almost miraculous results on the basis of the Biblical promise in Malachi 3:10. We looked it up:

Bring ye all the tithes into the storehouse . . . and prove me now herewith, said the Lord of hosts, if I will not open you the windows of heaven, and pour you out a blessing, that there shall not be room enough to receive it.

Frankly, we were at a loss to explain these stories. We don't believe that God necessarily rewards good people with material success: the most God-like men in history have been poor. And the whole point in giving is lost if there's a chance of getting more back in return.

We wrote to several religious groups for information about tithing. The idea of giving to charity, we learned, is found throughout the world. The Moslem, for example, has a proverb: "Prayer carries us half-way to God, fasting brings us to the door of His palace, and alms gain us admission."

But it was probably Jewish genius that first recognised the principle of systematic, proportionate giving. The tithe was designed to remind the ancient Jew at regular intervals that "All things come of thee, and of thine own have we given thee." In ancient Israel the first crops harvested, the first-born animals, were dedicated to God, to underline the priority of spiritual values.

Whether people give ten per cent or five per cent or 20 per cent, whether they tithe to the church or to secular charities, the experience has seemed to change their lives. We heard many stories of people who tithed and got rich.

John D. Rockefeller's mother persuaded him to give part of his first salary to charity. Later he tithed millions.

We learned that the founders of many successful businesses, such as Heinz's foods, Vick's Vaporub, Stanley Home Products, Quaker Oats, were men who tithed.

One friend wrote us: "Never having tithed before this year, I am continually amazed that we are enjoying the same standards necessary to the happiness and health of our family. I cannot truthfully say we 'gave up' anything in order to tithe. Our lives are fuller now and our blessings too numerous to count."

There was no doubt about it, tithing did something for people. So one Friday evening we subtracted ten per cent from our pay cheque and wrote out a cheque to the March of Dimes. We had good reasons for wanting to support that drive. But to each other we admitted that we were also curious to see whether after tithing for a year, we might have more money in the bank than we had then.

At the end of six months we came very close to abandoning the whole programme. The tithe was a big hunk out of our income and the choice of a charity once each week was a really important decision. We had let our tithing money accumulate for well over a month, until the total seemed like more than we could afford to give away, more than we would have spent at one time for anything else. It gave us a panicky feeling of over-spending.

We talked it over with members of the family and with friends. One neighbour suggested, "Why not wait until your children are grown and you are making a little more?" Another said, "Nobody gives ten per cent any more. They can't afford to. Besides, a lot of your taxes go to help other people. The Government does your tithing for you."

This, we found, is largely true. Today the Government spends nine times more than all other sources combined for what used to be considered 'private' charity: handicapped people, old people, orphans, the blind, the unemployed, etc. And on the other hand, George Gallup estimates that only three per cent of the population of this country tithe their incomes today. Most people, far from giving ten per cent, barely manage to squeeze out two cents on the dollar for voluntary giving.

We would have written the whole thing off, then and there, if it were not for one significant fact: tithers like tithing. Not once had we heard of anyone who began to tithe and then gave it up.

A Tulsa, Oklahoma, family wrote in their church bulletin: "Like most households we are cutting all possible corners. But our weekly tithing is the one thing we wouldn't think of cutting." Mr. Hartley S. Laycock, owner of a hotel in Cocoa, Florida, told us: "You can go quite broke tithing. I did, but I'm still a tither."

Another friend said, "There's all the difference in the world between handing over money because you have to and giving it voluntarily. When I'm making out my tax return, I hold out on every penny I legally can. But every time I can give a little more than ten per cent to my chuch, I do. I get a bigger kick out of giving a dollar to a blind accordionist than out of all the taxes I've ever paid."

We decided to continue tithing for another six months. But we still wondered what these people see in tithing that gives them so much enjoyment. Most of the tithers we know are not well-to-do; they are people to whom giving means sacrificing. And most tithers do not wait, as we were advised to, until they are earning a good income. Depression years abound with stories of families who tithed on very low incomes.

For most people, tithing doesn't mean money in the bank. However, during the second six months of our experiment we discovered some of the things it can mean. Four things happened to us: 1. We discovered the new *joy in giving*. Before we started tithing we were giving spasmodically. We had to wrench each dollar from our budget with a backward glance at the new pair of shoes the baby would need next month. Each time the woman from the Community Chest knocked at the door was an occasion for alarm, for hurried consultation and reluctant, probably not-too-gracious doling-out of money.

But when we agreed to set aside a definite sum for giving, we found that we no longer thought of it as a sacrifice. At first we opened a separate bank account for our tithe money. But now, to prevent it from accumulating again and tempting us to spend it, we mail out our weekly tithe cheque the day the family wage earner gets paid. We have learned not to think of this money as ours. We do hold on to the fun of deciding which cause we will give it to among those we have always wanted to help.

Tithing makes it easier to give, makes it easier to say no. We have found that when we regularly set aside a fixed portion of our income we can decide for ourselves what charities we most want to support and then say no to the others without feeling guilty.

2. We discovered a new *joy* in having money. It is as if, by the expansive act of giving, we chase away the spectre of the bottom dollar which has worried rich men, as well as poor, to their graves.

3. We achieved a new *sense of balance*. In order to find that weekly ten per cent for charity, we had to manage our budget more judiciously than before. We cut out negligent and wasteful spending habits that we hadn't previously noticed. Once we started using ten per cent of our income for truly important purposes, we took money more seriously, and the remaining 90 per cent seemed to go farther.

Paradoxically enough, the easing of tension over money matters that comes with tithing is just what a lot of men need to help them earn more money. The *Harvard Business Review* reported not long ago the importance of inner calm in making a success in the business world. The discipline of tithing is certainly one of the most potent devices for abolishing money worries and achieving this balance. Someone has said that in order to get out of debt it is necessary to tithe.

A 45-year-old editor who has been tithing for only a few years wrote us that the first change he noticed was that the top of his desk, which had been the office eyesore, suddenly became neat and orderly. Because his personal book-keeping had to be more systematic, he learned to be more orderly and efficient at the office. In time this was reflecting in his earnings.

It is easy to see why money, picked in study after study as the first cause of husband-and-wife arguments, often ceases to be a source of friction in tithing homes.

4. Finally, and most important, we experienced a *strengthening of religious faith*. We seemed to have a firmer grasp on the idea of God and love among men. Having invested a little money in the premise that there is more to life than material possessions, we found the idea itself more substantial.

This is not to say that giving away ten per cent pays one's debts to the world. Tithing is valuable as a token, a symbol of the fact that we recognise this indebtedness and are doing something about it. To stand up straight, to face the world with assurance and peace—these are the real rewards of tithing.

Words I Live By

by WILLIAM NICHOLS

> *"For eleven years I have been asking other people to express their 'Words to Live By',"* says the Editor of This Week *magazine. In this article, the tables are turned and Mr. Nichols is given a chance to express himself on a subject very close to his heart.*

As a layman, I am not sure I know just what is meant by the term 'religious experience', nor do I think I have the right to use it in this case. And yet I do know that the words I am going to give you 'came' to me, like a miracle, at a time when I was in very great trouble. I know, too, that they lifted me out of trouble. And, ever since, they have been with me, guiding and helping.

To tell the whole story would be too long and too personal. It is enough to say that it happened a long time ago. It was during one of those 'down' periods which, I suppose, come to everybody at some point—a period when everything goes black, and one feels paralysed by doubt, self-pity and fear.

Whether I heard the words, or saw them, I cannot say. All I know is that there was a moment when I suddenly became aware of them, and felt them *inside me* with an almost luminous intensity—and that moment was a turning point in my life. Since then these words have been always with me—a steady, unfailing source of courage and inspiration. I treasure them partly for what they say; partly because I think of them, truly, as a gift from God.

The words? Here they are:

"*Try to get through to help the other people.*"

These are such simple plain-Jane words. So homespun and ordinary. Yet in my case, at least, that is what gives them power. Somehow they seem to fit me and my everyday life and problems. In them there is nothing learned or 'literary' or far away. But there *is* a sort of four-fold lift in them.

1. First, the word—'*try*'. To me it seems to say: "Look, you aren't supposed to be perfect; you're supposed just to do your best, to make an effort—in short, to *try*—and if sometimes you fail, as all men do, then you can still try, and try again."

2. Next—'*to get through*'. That has a double meaning. First, it means 'get through' in the sense of growing up, of finishing, or having done with, all those childish doubts, fears and self-worries which hamper an immature personality. Second, 'get through' means also to break *through* in the sense of overcoming, or bursting out from that tight confining wall of selfishness and egotism which cuts so many of us off from the world and from each other.

3. The next words—*'to help'*—speak for themselves. They sum up the whole idea of losing yourself, of forgetting yourself, for someone or something else.

4. And whom shall we help? Why, of course—*'the other people'*. These closing words mean very much, for they wipe away the idea that anybody is higher or better or holier than anybody else. And the task, the challenge, the opportunity which God gives us, over and over, day after day, is the chance to *help one another*. It is the greatest grace there is.

These then are my Words to Live By: *'Try to get through to help the other people'*. Since I first heard them, I know with an absolute conviction that my only true moments of happiness, fulfilment or success have come on those occasions when I have been able to feel their message: to forget myself (that is, 'get through') and then to 'help the other people'.

Flames that Lick the Iron Curtain

by ROBERT MONTGOMERY

The final answer to communism lies not in force of arms or economic pressures but in the tiny fires of a greater ideology than Marx ever dreamed of . . .

ALL men of good will readily admit they are against grafters, gangsters, Communists.

If I have learned anything in my attempts to expose these Godless scuttlers of our way of life, it is this: to be *against* evil is never enough. We must be *for* the answer to evil.

And the answer is not one big blazing action, but many little ones, fought on many different fronts—usually by unsung people who believe like giants.

Such a giant is Ethar Milliken, a Marine farmer. I would like to tell you his story.

With his huge bare hands Milliken personally beat at the flames of a raging forest fire that threatened farm property around Kennebunkport, Maine, back in 1947. For several days and nights Ethar battled the flames until exhausted.

Milliken's condition made complete rest necessary the following winter. Doctors said he would never again be able to work on his land the way he did before—from sun-up to sun-down. It was his heart.

As he lay there in his farmhouse bed he did not curse the darkness of his day. He looked back into the valley at yesterday and over the mountain to tomorrow.

Oh, there had been hard times. Once almost all his cattle had been wiped out by disease. Several times he had been forced to borrow money to start all over again. But there had been good years, too. He now had two farms. Surely, God had been good to him.

"What can I do to repay my debt to Him?" Ethar asked himself.

And in asking, he little realised that he was starting a chain of events that would one day affect people he did not know in far off Estonia, behind the Iron Curtain.

"Two farms are too many for one man," he thought to himself. "One could easily be used to help those in need. But, who? And how?"

Milliken's first thought were of those who had suffered terrible tribulations during the war in Europe. What better way to show his gratitude to God and country than to give his farm for the use of those who wanted to build a new life in America? Why, whole families could live there—to learn about farming and American freedoms.

It would be called Freedom Farm. After exploring the idea further, he decided it would be best if an agency administered the project. The farm was turned over to the United Baptist Convention of Maine, and through this organisation, Freedom Farm became a state-wide project with co-operation from the Federal Displaced Persons Bureau.

The community caught Ethar's enthusiasm. With true New England thoroughness, housewives scrubbed the farmhouse floors; husbands painted and papered walls. A crew of ministers shingled the roof. The Baptist Youth Fellowship raised funds for a team of horses; a church in near-by Farmington Falls gave the first cow.

In June 1949, the first foreign family moved into Freedom Farm: Ants Parna, his wife, Agnes, and ten-year-old daughter, Lembi. The Parnas had fled from Estonia just in time to miss being drafted into a Russian work camp. For days they travelled by foot, begging food wherever possible. For a week they travelled by hiding in a freight car. At night Parna would sneak out and forage for potatoes, which they ate raw. Little Lembi nearly went blind from malnutrition. Finally they reached an American camp in the U.S. zone of Germany. Soon came the invitation to Freedom Farm.

Parna, however, had been a supervisor in an Estonian shoe factory. He knew nothing about farming. Strangely enough, this factor proved a disguised blessing. The Parnas arrived too late for the planting season. A drought, which followed, raised the price of hay. On the unplanted acres of Freedom Farm hay grew plentifully, nourished by water below the surface.

Three ministers from near-by towns, Archibald Craig, Chauncey Stuart, and Harold Bonell, gathered in a bumper hay crop, worth $2,500, and the plan to make the farm self-supporting was off to a good start.

Soft spoken Ethar Milliken was not at all surprised. "God is taking care of these people," he said.

In July 1949, a dedication service was held at Freedom Farm to honour the 'Americans-to-be' (a name Baptists prefer to D.P.s).

Mrs. Parna was asked what she thought of her adopted country. She replied, "Happy land!" Then grinned broadly.

The Parnas remained at Freedom Farm for over a year, the shoemaker becoming a competent farmer. Soon it was apparent that they not only could earn their bread by themselves, but also be an asset to any community. Parna then obtained employment in Illinois, making room for another family. Since then, 25 other Americans-to-be have 'graduated' from the farm.

The Parnas, Wowks, Gontschars, Milenkas, Wolotchajs —these are some of the Ukranian and Estonian people who found the answer to Communism on a farm in Maine, thanks to a real twentieth-century minute-man, Ethar Milliken.

Spiritual Commandos

by LEE H. BRISTOL, JR.

> Would you like to mobilise yourself to do God's work? Here's an article which tells you how to do it.

A FRIEND of mine, Wallace Speers, was waiting for a train in Pennsylvania Station one afternoon. Near him stood a man whose shoulders sagged and whose face needed a shave. Two British sailors approached Wallace and asked the way to the information booth. After Wallace had directed them, the unshaven man, near-by, walked over to Wallace. "Who were those men?" he asked.

"They were British sailors," said Wallace.

"Are you a British sailor?"

"No; what makes you ask that?"

"I thought you had something in common with them," said the man. "You're not like the others around here. You talk friendly."

Wallace replied that the city was full of friendly people who do a lot of good and yet never make headlines.

"Maybe so," said the man, who then proceeded to tell Wallace his whole life's story. He had committed a crime, was sentenced to twenty-five years in jail, and after serving fifteen years got out for good behaviour. "I'll bet you wish now you hadn't spoken to me," he said finally.

"No," said Wallace. "I don't see why. You've paid your debt to society and are a free man again."

The man looked at Wallace. "Say, will you do something for me?"

Wallace thought, 'Here it comes. Here comes the touch.'

"There's not a soul in this whole wide world who cares whether I live or die," said the man. "For a couple of weeks would you mind just thinking about me?"

To Wallace, this was one of the most pathetic statements he had ever heard. Of course, he has thought about that man many times since. It also made him realise how many lonely, desolate humans he probably came in contact with each day.

Wallace Speers is Vice President of a large New York department store. He is also Chairman of the Layman's Movement for a Christian World, an international non-denominational organisation whose purpose is to inspire laymen everywhere to search for a greater understanding of God and to find more effective ways of applying Christian principles to their everyday lives.

There are thousands of laymen—men and women—here in America today who are honestly trying to live their faith on a round-the-clock basis. They are not just 'do-gooders', but people who feel Our Lord is counting on them to do His work.

We call these people 'spiritual commandos', because they are mobilised and ready to do a job for God. It may mean driving 100 miles to visit a man in prison, or visiting the family of a boy who got in trouble in the big city, or it may mean just calling on the new family that moved into town. Most important, is that these 'commandos' don't have to wait for a special assignment from the Laymen's

Movement in New York which has their names and addresses. They look, near at hand, for a job they can do as active Christians.

A business man, who works across the street from me in New York, is a great believer in the fact that God will sometimes throw a rather unlikely assignment his way.

"No matter how unlikely this assignment, I simply can't dismiss it as not intended for me, because I can't be sure," he says.

One day, for example, his telephone rang. At the other end was a displaced person, a D.P., whom he had never met.

"I don't know you," he said, "but I've heard that you try to do a lot for your church and I've read about you. Well, I'm trying you as a last shot in the dark. There are 86 political prisoners in Italy who should have been released at the end of the war who are still locked up. Nobody seems to be able to do anything about them."

"Well," said my friend, "I'm just in the dry-goods business here in New York. What do you expect me to do?"

"I know that you once met the Pope. Won't you write to him?"

Well, my friend, who happens to be a Presbyterian, said he would think about it. He turned to other things at his desk, but the plea from this unknown man nagged at him. Finally, he wrote to the Vatican.

Two weeks later the D.P. called again. He was almost hysterical.

"I don't know what you did, sir," said the man, "but 84 of the 86 prisoners have been released!"

And sure enough, about a week later came a letter from the Vatican saying that my friend's letter had called a situation to their attention of which they had not been aware. Whereupon, through their intercession with the Italian Government, 84 of the 86 prisoners had been released. The other two prisoners were to have their cases reviewed.

You see what I mean? Often the sky is the limit for what an ordinary person can do. As this same friend puts it, "Lee, you can do just about anything for good you want, if you don't mind who gets the credit."

Beauty Secret of a Plain Girl . . .
by MURIEL SANATSAN

And with this secret came the formula for happiness.

ONE of the most radiant and best loved women I ever knew was also the plainest. In time I came to know the secret of her charm.

When Rachel Dow was still a small child here in New Ipswich, she went to visit her grandmother. She was, at that time, self-conscious, inhibited, and morose. When her grandmother was alone with her, she said in quiet, deliberate tones, "Rachel, you're mortally plain. I think you are the plainest girl I have ever seen. No—don't turn away. Sit down and listen to me. You are going to hear these words all your life; and I want to tell you something that people who are beautiful do not often know. I want you to understand how wonderful it is that you are so plain.

"In the first place, I want you to remember that plainness is nothing to be ashamed of, if you are born that way. You didn't make yourself plain—God did. And why, do you suppose? *So that you might better discover the secret of happiness!*

"Happiness, my child, lies in sharing the lives of others. No one is happy who thinks of himself alone. When you attract people's attention this will give you a chance to enter into their lives and bring them joy. In bringing joy to others, you will forget yourself and you will find the only lasting happiness.

"Whenever you see yourself in a mirror and realise your plainness, whenever you hear people say, or feel they are thinking, 'Goodness, isn't that girl plain!', Promise me you will smile and say to yourself, 'God and I have a secret!'"

I was present on the wharf one summer day, awaiting the arrival of a steamer. I saw Rachel come on to the pier, surrounded by a group of laughing young people—Rachel was all of 60 now. A woman who stood beside me exclaimed, "Mercy! Isn't that woman plain!"

Rachel overheard, turned, and flashed a radiant smile in our direction and, recognising me, came over to greet me. Then she said to the stranger at my side, "I don't recall seeing you here before. You must be a newcomer to our little town. I hope you're going to be happy here and that you will grow to love it as we do who come here year by year."

When she turned away, the stranger said to me, "Why, she's lovely, isn't she?"

Yes, Rachel, the Lord made you plain so that you could bring happiness to others as well as receive it yourself.

Accept the Challenge of Your Church

HAVE you ever heard this hackneyed, old statement?

"I can pray in the woods or on the golf course just as effectively as I can in church."

In most cases it is employed as a rather lame excuse by a person who doesn't want to bother with attending church. One can, of course, pray to God anywhere, but there never has been, nor probably ever will be, any better place to worship the Lord than in a church. It is the Lord's home, built and consecrated to His glory, and if nothing else it is a mark of respect for one to visit Him in it.

Also there has never been a better method devised for increasing one's personal faith than through direct participation in a church's programme. I don't mean simply going to hear the minister's sermon, but rather the act of worship in a quiet sanctuary, studying the Bible, receiving the Sacraments, listening to sacred music or joining in vital prayer and fellowship groups which many churches offer. The accumulated wisdom and spiritual experience of thousands of years is available to people through these programmes.

If you want to get complete medical treatment you go to a hospital. If you want to get the soundest and deepest spiritual help you go to a church. That's what it is for. It is there for you, ready to help you as it did the people in the following articles.

Norman Vincent Peale

Inside Our Home

by MRS. BILLY GRAHAM

> *What kind of family life do people expect of their minister? Here's a glimpse into the home of one of America's greatest preachers.*

ONE of the peculiar things about living in a preacher's family is the way strangers expect to see halos shining from all our heads. I say strangers. Our friends know better. They've seen little Franklin bite his sisters; they've seen Virginia and Anne and Ruth shouting or perhaps scrapping out on the front lawn. Our friends are fully aware that, for all our striving to make God the centre of our home, life in the Billy Graham household is not a matter of uninterrupted sweetness and light.

And it's not just the children. Our friends might very well have heard me moan to my husband Bill, about how I can never muster enthusiasm for doing dishes three times a day for a family of six. I love being a wife, mother, and homemaker. To me it is the nicest, most rewarding job in the world, second in importance to none, not even preaching.

But I don't like washing dishes.

To me there is no future in doing the dishes, nothing creative. And they are always there after each meal. I've even tried placing a little motto on the window sill above my sink. It's a motto I've had ever since high school, and it says: Praise and Pray and Peg Away. I made my dissatisfaction with the dishes a definite prayer concern and still I couldn't seem to dig up much enthusiasm.

But, as so often happens, my prayers were answered in an unusual way. I took sick at Christmas time. It was Bill, then, who had to take over and do the dishes.

What did Bill give me for Christmas?

An electric dish washer.

That's not the end of the story. When Dr. James Stewart of Edinburgh was in Montreal this summer, we were discussing housekeeping as a divinely appointed task, and he told of visiting a Scottish kitchen. Over the sink were these words:

"Divine service will be conducted here three times daily."

Bill and I do try to make our daily duties a divine service. Take, for instance, the job of disciplining the children. We try whenever possible to deal with our children's waywardness in terms of the Bible. I remember one time when Virginia, our oldest, who is ten, had to be disciplined. I've forgotten what the trouble was now. But that day I took heed of the proverb: Spare the rod and spoil the child.[1] Virginia was sweet as sugar for three days after that, and then she came to me and asked:

"Mother, why'd God ever create the devil and make me bad?"

It was a good question, although actually it's not too hard to answer. We talked about temptation. We talked about how if there were no evil, there'd be no test of our love for God. And we talked about the best ways to fight back, with prayer and with long talks with Christ.

The question of our relation to Christ is, of course, a very serious one in our house. When I say serious, I don't mean long-faced. You aren't long-faced when you talk over a problem with a good friend. But from the time they were first able to talk, we have tried very hard to teach our children that Christ is their personal Friend as well as their Saviour, And then, having prepared the soil, we let them grow in their own relationship to Him.

We try to start this relationship with the children's first nightly prayers. One time Franklin, who is three, was disciplined for continuing to pick the cat up by its tail,

[1] *Proverbs* 13. 24.

and that night he said in his prayers: "Please help Mommy to be a good Mommy and not shut me in my room any more."

These first prayers aren't ridiculous in the sight of a child, nor in the sight of the Lord. They are a fine beginning. In time, we try to show our children, by our own example, the different ways to live close to God throughout the day.

With four small children, the unexpected is always happening, like the time I heard little Ruth, who is four, break into a scream outside. I ran to see what the matter was and found her older sister smacking her first on one side of the face and then on the other.

"What on earth's going on?" I asked the other child.

"I'm just teaching her the Bible, Mommy, to turn the other cheek when she gets slapped."

It took quite some time to straighten that out.

Nothing is ever rigid around our house. For one thing, Bill's away so much of the time. Then, we always seem to be having visitors, both expected and unexpected. We even have a small zoo to keep track of. We don't count the temporary boarders like minnows and frogs and lame birds. As permanent guests we have a canary and a 'budgie', two patient and long-suffering cats, one of whom is so ugly we call her Moldy and a dog, an enormous Great Pyrenees called Belshazzar. Because he eats so much he reminds us of Belshazzar's Feast in the Old Testament.

Anyhow, with the four children and the animals, with guests coming and going, with travel, Bill's work, and just the normal household emergencies, a regularly scheduled time for worship is a bit difficult. Of course, we try hard to have morning family devotions and evening prayers, and always we have grace before meals. But I've long wished for a regularly scheduled private devotion period that makes a person feel he is living in the presence of God.

For years now I've found two substitutes:

One is day-long Bible reading which seems as natural to

the kids as my preparing meals. The Bible stays open in the kitchen or around the house all day, and whenever there is a spare moment, I enjoy a few minutes with it. When Bill is away and there is a problem, I find a lot of help in Proverbs. Proverbs has more practical help in it than any ten child psychology books put together. The 31 chapters in Proverbs and the 31 days of the month fit hand-in-glove.

Then there is prayer. Since we can't always seem to find one set-aside time, both Bill and I have learned what Paul meant when he wrote: *Pray without ceasing.*[1] I heard of a lady once who had six children and a very small home. She had no place for privacy. Whenever life got too hectic, she just pulled her apron over her head and the children knew she was praying and quieted down.

I don't do that myself, although I think it's a fine idea. Instead, as I'm busy around the house, dusting, making beds, cooking, sewing—whatever has to be done—I think of Christ as standing beside me. I talk to Him as to a visible friend. This is part and parcel of our daily lives so that keeping close to God becomes as much part of our children's training as keeping clean.

Sunday, we feel, should be a day set apart. It is a family day for us, but even more it's a day when we try to learn to know God better. It can be the most interesting experience in a child's life. We don't allow our children to play with their other playmates on Sunday, preferring it to be a family day. But we do have story books and colouring books, puzzles and games, all about the Bible. And we have special treats, like candy and soda, which they're not allowed to have on the other days. And we go up to our mountain cabin for the afternoon and sometimes for the night.

All in all, we have a wonderful time with no one but the family around, and somehow on Sunday there is a minimum of bedeviling and a maximum of very enjoyable companionship.

[1] *I Thessalonians* 5. 17.

It seems to Bill and me that the word 'enjoyable' would somehow be missing if we tried to go too fast with the spiritual growth of our children, with their halo-growing as it were. We believe spiritual growth can't be forced without raising a brood of little hypocrites. We prepare the soil and plant the seed, and water and weed and tend the plant faithfully. But it is "God that giveth the increase."[1] We're willing to take our time and let growth come from the inside, through Christ; not merely from the outside, through our puny efforts.

Yet, even if the motto I have out in the kitchen doesn't apply too well to dishes, it does apply to children and the problem of growing halos. Maybe the best thing, after all, is to Praise and Pray and Peg Away. The halos will take care of themselves.

How We Rediscovered Sunday

by GLENN FORD

> *What happened when a famous film star, known for his he-man rôles, became a Sunday School teacher's assistant.*

TWELVE years ago I married one of the most famous dancing stars in Hollywood. Today I am married to a Sunday school teacher. I haven't changed wives, either. I am still married to the glamorous Eleanor Powell. What's more the change in my wife's rôles, far from dimming the drama in our lives, has led us both to a richer experience.

The truth is that since our son, Peter Newton Ford, arrived ten years ago, both Ellie and I have found God in a new way.

In the beginning, neither Ellie nor I was a stranger to God. I think we had always tried to be 'good' people in His

[1] *I Corinthians* 3. 7.

sight. Ellie was raised a staunch Presbyterian, and I taught in the Episcopal Sunday school for a while after I graduated from high. Then, although we had not yet met, the same thing happened to us that seems to happen to a lot of people.

We just got too busy. Ellie was breaking into musical comedy in New York. I was making screen tests in Hollywood and appearing on Broadway. Almost without my noticing the change, Sunday wasn't church day any more. It was a day of rest. No performance. No audience. No tension. It was old-clothes day, read-and-sleep day.

For myself, I honestly believed that skipping church wouldn't dim my faith in God or make any difference in my relationship to Him. Occasionally, if I felt a personal need, as I did when my father passed away, I still went to church and came away strengthened, refreshed.

Dad's passing when I was 22, left me more deeply disturbed than I would confess. I couldn't shake off my sorrow and loneliness. Still close to the church habit, I walked around New York one gloomy Sunday and finally entered a church at random. The minister read from the 14th chapter of John: *Let not your heart be troubled: ye believe in God, believe also in me. In my Father's house are many mansions* . . . I have heard those words since—in Westminster Abbey, on the deck of the U.S.S. *California* when I was in the Marine Corps—always with the same feeling that they reached out to answer a personal need. That morning in New York was the first time their tremendous promise penetrated my consciousness, and I left the service filled with such peace as I had not known in many weeks.

Now, would any man wittingly turn his back on such a source of help? You wouldn't think so. But my immediate need had been met, and Sunday once more became a day of rest.

Then, after Ellie and I had been married for two years, along came Peter.

Our own re-education had begun.

Mine started almost at once. I had to begin to practice what I preached about table manners, and opening and closing doors for ladies, being alert in matters of honesty, neatness, the use of the English language. Peter's mother pointed out very firmly that we couldn't expect young Peter to "do as we say and not as we do".

Then Peter was enrolled in Sunday school in the Presbyterian Church of Beverley Hills. Or I should say Peter and Glenn and Ellie were enrolled. For could I say: "Run along, little man, and learn about God. Dad will sleep"?

Obviously not. Furthermore our Sunday school encouraged parents to sit in the back of the church while their young were being instructed.

We didn't exactly study their lessons with them, but I found myself learning other things. I learned that, in neglecting church, I had been missing something, that church could act as a catalyst between God and me, help to keep Him front-and-centre in my consciousness, increase my awareness of Him in daily living. I found that forming part of a congregation meant a closer tie with my fellow man, a giving, a sharing, as well as taking. Gradually I realised that, while I'd had no complaints before, things seemed to work more smoothly; I felt better; and I could only believe this stemmed from an increased vigour in my religious life stimulated by having Peter take us to Sunday school.

Perhaps the finest thing I learned was to watch with humility the fulfilment that can come from accepting Divine direction.

When Ellie decided to marry me and give up her career for family life and motherhood, I'll admit to moments of wondering if it weren't a shame that all my wife's wonderful talents should be reserved only for Peter and me and our immediate circle. Knowing how much real pleasure her dancing had given thousands, I sometimes felt that it was selfish of me to stand by and let her hide her light under a bushel of household duties.

But Ellie seemed sure that her decision was the right one and that if she were doing the Lord's will, a way would open up which would enable her to blend her professional talents with her family duties. Without her seeking it, without tension or struggle, a new opportunity did unfold which was part and parcel of our family life and through which she has reached a new audience of millions.

The seed was small and it grew naturally. One morning I dashed into Sunday school just under the wire to find Ellie leading the singing. Obviously she was enjoying it and so were the kids. Shortly afterwards she began serving as a substitute teacher then took a regular class of her own.

That was eight years ago and she has yet to miss a single Sunday. Never have I seen her inspire a Broadway audience the way she inspires those youngsters. They don't miss any Sundays either. And soon, on week days the neighbourhood kids were flocking around demanding Bible stories. She was, in theatrical terms a 'natural'. Nor was I the only one to notice it.

Over a year ago she was asked to teach her Sunday school class on television. We had both turned down TV offers before. Again Ellie said "no", this time for a different reason. She felt her former professional status might make suspect her appearance before the public in this new rôle. It took our own minister, Dr. Sam Allison, and the Reverend Clifton E. More of the presbytery quite a while to persuade her.

Once persuaded, she went into action. She added several children to her group to include all denominations. We hired a bus, and right after her regular class in church, off we went to the television station.

Technically, now I produce my wife's show. Nominally I'm supposed to "obtain suitable guests, write and produce", but actually I load the bus, brush hair and straighten ties, or provide an escort to and from the drinking fountain.

Whenever I try to summarise exactly how this all happened to us, I find myself turning to my star performer. At the close of each TV performance, Ellie shares with every listening parent the secret for happier living that our own son Peter taught us, when he took us to Sunday school.

"Stay with your children," she suggests. "Play with your children more. Above all, pray with your children more."

The Chain Around My Neck
by JIMMY DURANTE

There have been four special people in Jimmy's life and he has a special way of remembering them each day.

IT'S so tough down there on the lower East Side in New York where I was born we always think any kid who walks around with two ears is a hopeless sissy. In other neighbourhoods the truant officer chases the kids, in our neighbourhood we chase the truant officer. On the level, it's a real rough neighbourhood.

Later when I start playing the piano in Coney Island joints, I'm rubbing elbows with gangsters, gunmen, bootleggers and kidnappers.

None of that stuff dusts off on me hard enough to stick. For that I owe a lot to many people, but mostly to four special ones. To remind myself of what I owe them, and because I love them, I carry on a chain around my neck four little gifts they give me. I wear them so long they're like part of my flesh. I know they're part of me that isn't flesh. They're like four commandments that aren't listed with the big ten.

Every morning I put my fingers on the chain around my neck and I feel rich. I mean you can probably buy the four things and the chain for 50 cents and still get change. But I feel rich for what they give me in my heart.

One of these gifts is a medal of the Madonna. My pop give me that. He was a barber, and when I'm a kid he lets me lather up the faces of his customers. It's his hard-earned dollars, and there were never a lot of them, that learns me how to play the piano. Bartolomeo Durante, the barber, the kindest, gentlest man I ever know. In giving me the medal he teaches me the art of giving. If his customers don't have the price, he'd cut their hair anyway. To the day he died he wants to give away everything he has.

When he gets too old to barber he lives with my sister Lillian in Brooklyn, and he walks down the street and he passes out all the money he has to anyone who needs it. It gets so bad he can't carry any money with him. So I send it to Lillian and make her his banker.

You know, I don't think I ever see him mad a minute in his whole life. I'd like to be like him.

"Watch the friends you pick," he always says to me. "Some will steal your heart and your thoughts. Avoid them. You only pick the ones to whom you can *give* your heart and your thoughts."

I always try to.

The second gift on the chain around my neck is a medal of the Crucifixion. My wife, Jeanne, give it to me when we was married in 1921. We was married for 22 years. She died in 1943. Lord have mercy on her.

Her medal of the Crucifixion always reminds me of the art of forgetting and forgiving. Even how I met her reminds me of forgiving.

She came from Toledo, Ohio, and she's a very pretty girl. Pretty inside as well as outside. And she's a great singer. What a pair of pipes she has.

I'm working in an uptown joint in Harlem then, the

Alamo, and she drops in looking for a job. The boss eyes her, and says:

"Let's hear you sing. Go ahead, Jimmy, play the piano for her."

I resent that because I'm busy—I don't know what I'm busy about. But I feel busy. So I play a few blue notes and clinkers. She stops, and she's real angry, and she says:

"You are probably the worst piano player in the world."

"Them are the conditions that pervails," I say.

First she busts out laughing, and then she lights up the room with the shiningest smile I ever see.

So what do I do? I marry her.

Jeanne knows people and how weak-minded they get, and watching her heart work I learn what forgiveness is. One day she entrusts an acquaintance with some money. A slight loan, you might say. And when it's time to return it, the money isn't there. So the guy says he's sorry and tells her why he hasn't got it. Jeanne never asks him again.

"I feel resentment when I ask and he refuses," Jeanne says. "I don't want to feel resentment, so I'll never ask him."

I never want to feel resentment, so if anyone owes me anything I never ask either.

Jeanne is always telling me: "If anyone does something wrong to you they'll be more unhappy about it than you will. So forget and forgive."

I'm not proud—it takes a lot of time and trouble to keep even the smallest nose in the air.

The third thing on my chain is a St. Christopher's medal. To me it's the art of friendship. Through the years I learn it from my friends Eddie Jackson and Lou Clayton. Lou is around us still even though he died. But a stranger I still don't know and the St. Christopher medal keep reminding me of what friendship means.

I get the medal about six years ago. I'm ready to start a 17 day grind of one night stands across the country on a bond drive tour when Lou Clayton takes me to the doctor for a check-up. The last X-ray shows a polyp in my lower stomach.

So I'm elected for surgery. No tour. No radio. Nothing. But Al Jolson, Bob Hope, Red Skelton, and Frank Morgan took turns doing the radio show for me. That's what success really is, to have friends of that sort. Do the best you can. Stick with your friends, Pray they'll stick with you. The rest is in God's hands.

If I don't have that operation, that polyp could have gone malignant and I am in real trouble. God is really with me.

When they give me that shot in the arm, right before I go into the surgery, and I'm just about getting subconscious I feel someone touching my neck. When I wake up from the antiseptic I see this St. Christopher medal around my neck and I ask the nurse:

"Where does this come from?"

And she says: "Right before we took you up a nice lady with grey hair, dressed very nice, comes in, and kneels down, and says a prayer, and then slips this around your neck, and then she begs the doctor: 'Please doc, take good care of him,' and then she runs out."

Anyway I can never forget this stranger with the St. Christopher medal.

Before my mother dies over 25 years ago she gives me a little beat-up cross. That's the fourth gift on my chain. She wore it all her life, and when she gives it to me she says: "Never take it off, and God will always be with you."

It isn't true that I start each day with a song. That's second. I start each day with a prayer. That I get from Mom. She teaches me the art of believing. That's probably the greatest of the four commandments on my chain.

Oh, she teaches me all the commandments, all right, my mother. A saint. God have mercy on her soul. One time, I think I'm about five years old, I'm walking down the street with her, and we pass a vegetable pushcart. I just snitch a piece of corn; all the kids do. Two blocks later Mom turns around and sees the corn and asks me:

"Where did you get it?"

"Off the pushcart," I says.

She hauls me by the ear for two blocks all the way back to the pushcart and makes me explain to the pedlar and give it back. I am highly mortified. But that's her way of teaching me the commandments.

As a kid she tells me: "Without believing, you're nothing." And she points to one of the tough guys on the block: "He hasn't got God in his heart," she says. And she turns to a good guy like my father and says: "This one, he has God in his heart."

And we always follow her to church, without her asking, to find where God is. Even after she dies I still follow her.

For a while there's a time when I think I'm too busy to follow her, and during this time I'm helping Father James Keller; he's head of the Christophers. I am helping him make a movie, and he asks me:

"Going to church regular?"

I got to admit I miss here and there. "I been very busy," I alibi.

"You find the time," Father Keller says. "You find time for everything else."

He's real severe about it. Would you believe it? And there I am doing a picture for him for free.

But after that, when I think I'm too busy, I touch the beat-up little cross on the chain around my neck, and remember to follow my mother to where God is.

And you know the nicest thing about following my mother to where God is? I always feel it's like walking out of darkness into the sun.

A Medal for Freddie

by ROSALIND RUSSELL

> *An amazing story of adventure, a raftfull of survivors on the open ocean, and an agnostic.*

LANKY, greying Hans Christian Adamson was visiting us in Hollywood when we noticed the first strange turn in our old battle. We were at dinner, back in 1942. It was a long table. I sat at the head of it; Hans Adamson was at my right; and my husband, Freddie Brisson, sat at my left. We were all chatting, when suddenly Hans reached into his pocket and fished among his coins.

Now, Hans and my husband were close friends in spite of the 20 years difference in their ages. They were both officers in the Air Force. Hans Adamson was one of the best-read men I have ever known.

Hans was also an agnostic.

Not anti-religious; he was interested in religion, but there were things he could not accept with his rational mind. Back at his home, on the East Coast, he used to attend church occasionally with his wife, Helen, who was an Episcopalian. But we had the feeling it was more out of respect for her than for her beliefs. Hans often said he envied people who could believe without understanding. "But that's as far as I can go," he would tell us during our long talks about religion. "I try to understand your churches and your little medals and things. But I cannot. So I cannot believe."

That's why it struck us as so peculiar when Hans fished among his change that night and brought out a medal.

"Freddie," Hans said, and it seemed that his voice pitched a note higher than usual, "Freddie, I stopped at the PX and got you one of those new flying medals. St. Joseph of Copertino. I think he flew or something. You're going to do a lot of flying, and I want you to have this."

With that, the second strange turn occurred. My hand shot out. I grabbed Hans's sleeve. I spoke very impulsively. "No. Keep that yourself."

"Why?" Hans asked. "I don't want any medals. I got it for Freddie. He's a Catholic and he believes in these things."

I realised I had spoken sharply, and I tried to soften it down. "What I mean is, you keep it for now, Hans. You just keep it for now."

We all kind of looked at each other, and I tried to change the subject. The dinner party was ruined. But in my mind, I sensed a premonition that actually I had done the right thing . . . that Hans was trying to tell us something with that medal.

Three months later, Hans phoned my husband that he was going on a secret mission across the Pacific and that he would be coming out to California for a visit.

We all spent the day together in Beverley Hills. Hans kept saying that he felt nervous. He had never talked that way before. There is not a bit of cowardice in Hans Adamson yet he kept saying the trip had a fatality about it.

Frankly, we thought nothing about it at the time. But then, at six the next morning, the phone rang.

It was Hans.

"Will you do something for me? Will you call Helen and say good-bye again?"

I was puzzled why Hans didn't call his wife himself. At first I thought he was afraid of alarming her by calling so early. But I answered: "Of course I will."

Then, once more, Hans said something about the trip. And I at last saw that he had really called to seek help. Right out of the blue I sat bolt upright in bed.

"Hans, do you have that medal that you tried to give Freddie some time ago?"

Hans was silent for a moment, as if he didn't want to answer.

"Yes," he finally admitted, "I've got it in my pocket."

"Well. Now, mind you I don't think anything is going to happen. But if it does, if something should go wrong, you take that medal out and put it in your hand and hold on to it."

There was a prolonged silence. I thought I had offended Hans. When he did answer, it was with the single word:

"Yes . . ."

After he hung up, I couldn't get back to sleep.

"What's the matter?" Freddie asked.

I told him I felt something was going to happen. I wished I had explained more to Hans about the Catholic use of medals, how we don't claim special powers to the medal itself, how the medal helps us focus our prayers, reminds us of our need for prayer. But I had missed my chance.

We were about to get up when Freddie mentioned: "Oh, by the way, Roz. Hans has a rather famous companion for his trip across the Pacific."

"Yes?"

"Captain Eddie Rickenbacker . . ."

It was perhaps the most famous aeroplane crash in history. Captain Eddie Rickenbacker, Hans, and six others, on a secret mission, went down in the Pacific.

From Wednesday, 21st October 1942, until Saturday, we were more or less hopeful. We learned what had happened. The plane had missed its island destination in the night, probably through faulty instruments.

By the fourth day, most of my own personal hope had dwindled. By the end of the first week, I had given up all hope. The chances of surviving the crash for more than a few moments seemed slim to me. A week spent on a flimsy life raft under a tropical sun, with no protection, would surely kill any survivors.

But my husband thought Hans was still alive. Freddie

had that simple kind of trust I have seen so often, especially in men.

"You must understand," I said. "Hans is not a young man."

But even as I was saying this, Freddie whispered with great depth to his voice:

"He's alive. I know he is alive. He's getting strength from somewhere . . ."

I thought of the medal, and for a fraction of a moment almost believed.

Time began to be counted in weeks. The second week passed, and the third began. The search party was cut down in size. We knew that only a few routine patrol planes were continuing the endless task of searching for the tiny rubber rafts on the ocean. Eighteen days passed. Nineteen and twenty.

And then, suddenly, it was all over.

On the 21st day, the rafts were spotted. The headlines shouted, but we felt strangely quiet. As if we were being drained of the last of some sort of strength.

On the 22nd day, the rescues were made. We learned that Hans was still alive, although from the very first reports he was on the critical list. The men were kept in overseas hospitals for five weeks before they could be moved.

Then, just before Christmas, I got a call at the studio. It was from my husband, at the Air Base. The hospital plane was coming into San Francisco. Hans had sent a message that he wanted me to be there, that he had something that he wanted to tell me.

We saw Captain Rickenbacker first. He stepped off the plane, perhaps the thinnest man I have ever seen. His shirt stuck out inches, literally, from his neck. His 80-year-old mother was there to greet him. He walked towards her and she towards him for a few paces. Then they stopped. You could feel the pulses of emotion between them. I had to turn away, because it was something I could not watch.

I was told to get on the plane. Freddie and I climbed a ladder and were inside. I had never seen anything like it: so warlike and barren and canvasy. Hans was in bed. He looked worse than Rickenbacker.

I was so upset seeing him and remembering the old Hans, that I tried to keep the conversation on trivial things: welcome home, how good it was to see him alive. I had to say that, rather than how well he looked, because of course he looked anything but well.

Freddie looked at Hans and said: "I don't remember hearing about your hand."

The hand was bandaged.

"It's hurt a bit," Hans answered.

And with that he slowly removed the bandage.

There, cupped in his hand, was the medal.

From holding it in the same position for weeks, his hand muscles had frozen so that he could not straighten his fingers. The medal had worked its way into his flesh. Hans looked up at me.

"I didn't even let them take it away in the hospital."

The plane was silent while with his other hand Hans pried the medal loose. Then, softly, he spoke again.

"It's all right, Roz. I understand at last . . . May I give Freddie the medal now?"

Experience the Joy of Self-Surrender

"A PERSON isn't born a Christian. He's born again a Christian." To some people it might seem strange that these words were spoken by a cop who has been on New York's tough police force for over twenty years.

"When I get a problem I can't answer myself, I ask the Lord to help me."

You might be surprised to learn that this is one of America's most distinguished business executives speaking.

Each of these men, though vastly different from the other and in entirely different circumstances, discovered for himself the same key to a strong and abiding faith. That key is *self*-surrender, the giving in of himself to God so he can give out to people.

How do you surrender yourself? The stories in this section will help supply you with a blueprint for undertaking that task.

But first of all, don't be disturbed by that word 'surrender.' This does not mean retreat; it is a step forward. When you surrender yourself, you will usually be discarding a tired or unhealthy way of life for something new and invigorating. Try it—and see.

Norman Vincent Peale

The Crisis of Self Surrender
by SAMUEL M. SHOEMAKER

> Dr. Samuel Shoemaker, rector of Pittsburg's Cavalry Episcopal Church, is one of America's outstanding clergymen. Here are parts of his personal story, disclosing what he believes to be the key element in man's spiritual rejuvenation.

SHORTLY after my graduation from Princeton in 1916, I went to Peking, China, to instruct in a combination boys' school and Christian Association. I was told I would teach English, the Bible, and insurance.

"But I've never read a line about insurance in my life," I said in dismay.

"You read English faster than these Chinese schoolboys; so you're going to teach insurance," the school principal replied.

In my Bible class of 'inquirers', mostly young businessmen working in government services, we began with 25 members; the next week 17 turned up; and the third week, about 10. I soon became aware that the unhealthy condition of the class was due not only to my poor teaching, but also to the fact that I needed something more in my own life to offer them.

At this time there appeared in Peking a group of men who held meetings with both missionaries and businessmen, and told stories of great changes in people's lives. I asked one of these men to help a young Chinese businessman who was ripe for conversion to Christianity.

He only said, "Why don't you do it yourself?"

"Episcopalians don't work in this direct fashion," I answered.

"What's the trouble?"

Before we finished talking, I had the uneasy feeling that my own Christian dedication and commitment lacked a basic ingredient.

William James says that the *crisis of self-surrender* has always been, and must always be, regarded as the vital turning point of the religious life. In Peking I first faced that crisis. Yet I suspect that no man in this world, except our Lord Jesus Christ, ever surrendered himself absolutely.

After this talk, I spent a very uncomfortable evening of self-examination and tallied up my ineffectiveness at getting across to others the Christian message. When 17, for example, I wrote a religious book. It was utter, vaporous trash. Later there was the small summer congregation for whom I held services. Three people in that group met tragic experiences. Why? Partly because what religion I gave them was so general. The same pattern of failure kept following me. Individuals sought spiritual help which I could not give them.

There are people whose mechanical use of the church's spiritual means has rubbed a callus on their souls. I belonged in this class until I got down on my knees that night and surrendered as much of myself as I knew—my sins, needs, pride, joys, everything—to as much of Christ as I understood at that time.

Four elements went into that initial surrender.

The first concerned *a break with conscious wrong*. For example, I had been nursing a resentment. Remonstrating with the Lord I said, "Nine-tenths of this is the other person's fault." I think I heard Him say, "What about the one-tenth for which you are responsible?" I had to face up to God's will.

The second concerned daily morning *devotions*. I had tried this again and again, only to give it up in despair. Now I began taking a regular half an hour for Bible study and prayer (using a list of persons to pray for regularly). This is like a spiritual breakfast.

The third concerned *fellowship with other Christians*.

Power is generated in small groups meeting regularly. The early Christians moved and worked dynamically together, this way. Pray to be led to one person: here is your nucleus. In my case this was another Princeton man, Larry, who was himself just getting started on working spiritually with people.

The fourth concerned *witness*. Live germs are always contagious. I knew there was something missing when I could not make Christ live for other people.

The day after my own big decision, I felt strongly led to go to see this Chinese businessman myself.

When I rapped on his door, however, I hoped that he wouldn't be at home.

My heart sank when he said, "Come in." As I went over the threshold, I said to God, "Please tell me what to say." And it came to me quite clearly, "Tell him what has just happened to you."

I realised for the first time that I had not only a case to argue for the Christian religion but I also had a personal witness to give as to what that faith had begun to do for me in my own life.

More to my amazement than to his, perhaps, this young man made a Christian decision that day. And nearly every afternoon thereafter I would ask a Chinese boy to come to my house to talk. I couldn't speak Chinese, and they knew little English; but I found some places in the Chinese Bible which I marked for them to read when I wanted to make sure they would understand what I was saying.

The episode with the Chinese businessman made me realise that there is no substitute for hours of attention given to individual people. You can preach valuably to crowds; you can teach and experiment with small groups; but you don't really clinch it until you talk personally with individuals.

When I later became rector of Calvary Episcopal Church in New York City, a great new opportunity faced me to work with individuals on this basis. We started by gathering some people together every Tuesday noon to pray for the awakening of the parish. We prayed that the right people would come along to help us do the job.

Calvary Church became a spiritual centre for people with many different needs and backgrounds. Out of them we found many good workers and even staff members. In the nearly 27 years I was there, we also had about 80 full-time volunteer workers, seven days a week. Since coming to Calvary Church in Pittsburgh, I have endeavoured to further the same work with individuals begun in New York.

Does the initial decision of surrender last? No. You have to renew it every time you honestly pray.

Maybe you run into somebody looking for spiritual help. When you get it all sifted out, he or she needs to give his life as fully as possible to God. You realise that you cannot ask them to do this unless you are ready to do it again yourself. So you do it together. The Christian life is mostly a fellowship of sinners, who need forgiveness a great many times.

What is the most thrilling experience I've ever had? It's always one thing: to see somebody find Christ and faith. My 'most thrilling experience' happens every two or three days!

Thousands in our churches, today, are possessed of beliefs but not power. This is largely, I believe, because no servant of His, minister or layman, has ever lovingly and directly dealt with these people on this problem of self-surrender. The Church today has no greater business than to train tens of thousands of its men and women to do this.

Decision of the Heart

by BONNIE BONHIVER

> And it was a difficult decision. For how does a handicapped young girl know whether a man's attentions come from love or sympathy?

JERRY MITCHELL seemed surprised at my appearance on that cold bleak Valentine's Day back in 1950. I'm sure he pictured me as a frail, pallid creature who was facing life with one of those grave, weary smiles.

He had come to record an interview with me for his radio programme on Station WJOB at Hammond, Indiana.

"Now then," Jerry instructed after the equipment was in place, "I'll introduce the show first, then I'll ask you a few questions about yourself. Ready?"

I nodded agreement. With Jerry sitting beside me, smiling encouragement, my fear of the mike quickly faded. I went back seven years and told him of my life at seventeen—the dances, dates and the expectation of college—and then that dinner when the chair was accidentally pulled out from under me. At the time it was a painful fall, but didn't seem serious. Later my body became paralysed.

It was hard to find adequate words to describe to Jerry the first discouragement and despair I felt . . the struggle to learn how to hold a glass, brush my hair, then to knit, and finally to feed myself.

"How long did it take you to get on your feet?" Jerry asked.

"Nearly seven years. When I first tried to lift my body on all fours, I fell off the bed on to the floor. But within a month I could crawl to the foot of my bed and back. Then came the slow step-by-step process of advancing to wheel chair stage, then to a walker, to crutches and now to a cane.

"But I don't want anyone to think that I'm patting myself on the back, Jerry. I could never have made it alone. Hundreds of sympathetic, magnificent people helped me—my mother, the policemen who took me back and forth to the doctors in the squad car, and many others.

"The turning point came when I read of others who overcame difficulties by faith. I was suddenly filled with a desire to know God's will for my life. As I gradually gained confidence in myself and the power of God, I was given the incentive to fight back. I no longer feel that I am trying to conquer tragedy just for myself, but for everyone who would ever need to have hope."

The interview lasted only fifteen minutes, but Jerry stayed until after midnight. We toasted marshmallows and hot dogs in the fireplace and talked.

"I'm not handicapped, Bonnie," he said, munching his frankfurter reflectively, "but I want to bring inspiration and courage to people, too."

It was a wonderful evening. Two of us, both young, talking about our ideals, hopes and ambitions. Jerry's interests were in radio and television. I wanted to write, to share my experience with others.

Jerry began dropping in regularly after that. He loved to sit by the fireplace and talk about his work. I liked to see his enthusiasm and to watch his eyes light up when he got a new idea.

Then gradually a shift took place in our relationship. It made me glow inside, yet it frightened me. Perhaps I was afraid of being hurt, or that Jerry might confuse love and sympathy. I had already gone through one such experience. "I love you enough to take you just as you are," a suitor had told me.

I certainly didn't want that. My dream of marriage was where two could work together as a team, building together and helping others.

My father's death, then eight years of battling against my handicap, had knocked the giddy, schoolgirlish traits out of me. I knew love in the sense of concern, devotion and sacrifice. Drawing close to God had awakened me to a new kind of life where people found joy in giving rather than taking. I wanted to be sure that my husband felt the same way.

A week later Jerry asked me to marry him. I said no. He ignored my refusal. Night after night he would help me practise walking, then we would plan his radio talk together. I pasted inspirational articles and quotations in a scrapbook for him; occasionally I wrote a script for him. For the first time in eight years, I began to feel needed.

"Do you love me?" he asked one evening after I had again said no to his proposal.

Without looking at him, I nodded.

"Then you must have faith in me," he went on. "Because love means having faith. We can do much more together, for one another and for others, than we could ever do alone."

I finally agreed. So, on Thanksgiving Day, 1950, we were married in the First Unitarian Church here in Evanston.

Today, with Jerry's help, I manage all the work myself, even though I cannot yet walk without holding on to furniture. Washing dishes, making beds and making Jerry's favourite oatmeal bread have, one by one, become accepted again as normal.

Three times a week, we talk as a husband-wife team on his radio programme. It is exciting to feel that our efforts might touch other lives. On one recent programme we tried to show how God has a pattern for each life—as He certainly has for ours—and how the greatest happiness comes when we let ourselves be caught up in some higher purpose.

24 Words that Can Change Your Life

by HERBERT J. TAYLOR

A former president of Rotary International writes about the two dozen words which have changed not only his own life but others as well.

THE 24 words came to me as a direct answer to prayer. It was in the depression year of 1932. I had given up a good job to become president of Club Aluminum in Chicago, then a bankrupt company over $400,000 in debt. If it folded, 250 men and women would be thrown out of work.

To win our way out of this situation, I reasoned, we must be morally and ethically strong. I knew that in right there was might. I felt that if we could get our employees to think right, they would do right. We needed some sort of ethical yardstick that everybody in the company could memorise and apply to what we thought, said, and did in our relations with others.

When I get a problem I can't answer myself, I ask the Lord to help me. So one morning I leaned over on my desk, rested my head in my hands, and prayed.

In a few moments I reached for a white paper card and wrote down that which had come to me—in 24 words. Here it is:

THE FOUR-WAY TEST
1. Is it the TRUTH?
2. Is it FAIR to all concerned?
3. Will it build GOODWILL and BETTER FRIENDSHIPS?
4. Will it be BENEFICIAL to all concerned?

I decided to check everything that came up that day against the first question, "Is it the truth?" The first thing

I picked up was a copy of some advertising we were running. It ballyhooed our product as "the greatest cooking ware in the world". "We can't prove that," I said. "It just isn't true."

I called in the advertising manager, and we cleaned up the ads. We eliminated all superlatives from the copy. We stopped using words like 'better' or 'best' or 'finest' and simply stated the facts about our product.

After 60 days I talked it over with my four department heads—by faith, a Christian Scientist, a Roman Catholic, an Orthodox Jew, and a Presbyterian.

"Is this test contrary to anything in your faith?" I asked.

They all said no and agreed to memorise and use it. We asked everyone in the company to do the same.

Some time later one of our top salesmen came in to see me. "Mr. Taylor, this thing's going to hurt sales," he said. Our procedure was to sell a dealer as much as we could; loading him down with our products was considered good salesmanship.

"But that doesn't agree with Number Three—Will it build good will? nor Number Four—Will it be beneficial to all concerned?"

"Let's try selling according to the Four-Way Test, and in the long run it will be profitable," I suggested.

A little later our salesmen handed clients a calling card with the test questions printed on the back. "Of course, I can't live up to this perfectly, but I'd appreciate your help," a salesmen would say. "Whenever you find I'm not living up to it, let me know and I'll do my best to change."

Instead of persuading a dealer to take more than he needed, the salesmen sold only what the dealer thought he could dispose of, and then helped him to sell the merchandise.

Some time later we gave a job to a printer because his bid was about $500 under the others. When he delivered the order, he told us that he had made an error of $500 in his estimate. Could we see our way to making it up to him? We went into conference. To a firm deep in debt every penny counted. "We acted in good faith—let him take his loss," one executive said. "But that doesn't agree with Number Two—Is it fair to all concerned?" another broke in. Convinced it was an honest error, we gave the printer the $500. Had it not been for the test, I doubt that we would have.

We continued to follow the test, and with the new-won confidence of our dealers and customers, the business improved. Our volume increased.

After five years we paid off the $400,000 debt with interest. In the next 15, we distributed over a million dollars in dividends to stockholders. The moral and ethical benefits from the use of the Four-Way Test, however, are of greater and more lasting value than the material returns. It has helped us win friends and build confidence and good-will with those we contact in our relations in business and community life.

The Four-Way Test influenced my home life, too. One morning at breakfast my wife said, "Beverly is to be in a recital at school today, Herbert. Why don't you come?"

"Oh, I can't possibly. I'm just too busy," I said.

Then I thought, was I being fair to Beverly? And was neglect of home responsibilities beneficial to all concerned?

That afternoon they were surprised to see me show up at the recital, but they soon got used to having me. I witnessed Beverly's every appearance, whether in piano, oratory, or dramatics, and later, each of the recitals of her younger sister, Ramona, as long as they were in school.

One day in studying the Book of Jeremiah in the Bible, and realising that the Four-Way Test had come to me as an answer to prayer, I found the reason why the Four-Way Test covers all human relations so well. In Jeremiah, the ninth chapter, 23rd and 24th verses, we find the following: *Thus saith the Lord, Let not the wise man glory in his wisdom, neither let the mighty man glory in his might, let not the rich man glory in his riches: But let him that glorieth glory in this, that he understandeth and knoweth me, that I am the Lord which exercise loving kindness, judgment, and righteousness, in the earth: for in these things I delight,* saith the Lord. And there you have the fundamental principles involved in the Four-Way Test.

At a Rotary Club meeting a few years ago, I told about the Four-Way Test and how it had helped in our business. "Mind if I jot it down?" one man said, and several took out their pens and copied it. One of the members of the board of directors of Rotary International who was present asked if the organisation might use it to promote Rotary's objective of high ethical standards around the world. Today, nearly all the 411,000 Rotarians in 8,700 cities of 92 countries are familiar with it. It sits on the desks of over 100,000 of the leading business and professional men of America as a constant guide in their relations with others.

Some Rotarians in Japan felt that the test had helped them so much that they put it on posters and placed them in libraries, railway stations, and other public places. This gave Rotary the idea of introducing it to schools. It has now been introduced to schools in 22 countries of the world.

If with the aid of the Four-Way Test we can get the oncoming generation to think right, they will speak right and do right. If they speak right and do right, they will provide the future leadership of high moral character which the world so desperately needs.

The Strength of Kanoh
by STANLEY MANIERRE

> How the simple kindness of a Japanese guard during World War II changed the life of an American prisoner.

WHEN our B-24 hit the water, I was pinned down by the top turret. Yet, somehow I worked myself loose and out of the water-filled plane through the bottom hatch. Just as my lungs were about to burst, I came up beside the plane fuselage. Only four of our ten-man crew got out: pilot, co-pilot, bombardier and myself, the radio operator. The bombardier died later of his injuries.

We drifted four days on a life raft towards Saipan (then held by Japanese), where we were captured, flown to Yokohama and transferred to a prison camp outside of Tokyo. The date of our internment—29th May 1944.

Soon we were hearing B-29 bombers overhead, as day and night, they dropped fire bombs on Tokyo. Japanese guards showed their bitterness—except one, Kanoh-San.

Kanoh was our interpreter and spoke perfect English. He was different. There was a perpetual smile on his face and kindness in his heart. When our need for food and medical supplies were desperate, Kanoh would whisper, "I will try."

We were amazed that he would endanger his life to do this. When I discovered the reason, I never forgot it . . .

When the war ended, I returned to my home in Hartford, Connecticut, anxious to start a civilian career.

But first I felt an inner compulsion to visit the families of my bomber crew members who died in the crash. And from every family came this question, spoken or unspoken: "Did he die for something worthwhile?"

I was to think about this often, and at the same time,

ask myself, "Was I spared to do something worthwhile?"

Still uncertain about a career, I took a job as a salesman. One day our pastor, Reverend Melvin Prior of Hartford's Central Baptist Church, called me into his office. "Stan," he said, "did you ever think of going into the ministry?"

There was a silence for a few moments. I knew how Moses must have felt when he was first called by God to lead his people and said, "Who am I—slow of speech and slow of tongue—who will listen to me?"

"It's not for me," I replied. But the seed was planted.

In 1948 I was asked to go to the Annual Religious Education Conference held by our American Baptist Assembly at Green Lake, Wisconsin. On the closing night there was a consecration service on the point, a strip of land jutting out into the beautiful big Green Lake.

All the lights on the Assembly Grounds were extinguished for this service. The only light shone down from Judson Tower—a lighted cross—throwing its dazzling white reflection on the water below. The tower was invisible at night; only the cross stood as if suspended in midair. We stood facing that cross and singing "When I survey the wondrous cross, on which the Prince of Glory died, my richest gain I count but loss, and pour contempt on all my pride".

A great feeling of enthusiasm took hold of me, and, more than anything else, I knew I wanted to serve Christ. Could I do this best as a salesman, or a minister? To many, the answer would be, and should be, as a salesman. But for me it came out the ministry.

My choice of Andover Newton Theological School (outside Boston, Massachusetts) was fortunate because it was in near-by Cambridge that I met and later married Evelyn Cowan. After my graduation, the two of us worked as a team in the First Baptist Church of Hanson, Massachusetts.

But was this what God really wanted me to do? Was this the best answer I could give to the question, "Did they die for something worthwhile?"

From the beginning, I had a deep interest in the world outreach of the Christian Church.

There was also a picture engraved on my mind of prison camp and one man, Kanoh-San. For I had discovered two curious things about Kanoh before leaving Japan.

First, at the very time he was so kind to us, Kanoh's home had been bombed to shambles by American bombers.

Secondly, Kanoh in his youth had come under the influence of a Christian school, where he learned about the love Christ had for people. Love became a stronger force in Kanoh than fear of his superiors or the hate he could have felt for the people who destroyed his home.

What happened to Kanoh, multiplied by thousands of people in many areas, can change the world. I wanted to be part of this effort.

So three years ago my wife, myself, and our three youngsters left for Japan as missionaries of the American Baptist Foreign Mission Society. Our strength was Christ's words, *Lo, I am with you alway even unto the end of the world.*[1] We prayed that, as a family, we may have the quality of love that won Kanoh-San.

The events of the past years convinced me of one overwhelming fact: God has a plan for every individual, no matter how unpromising. We have the choice of resisting Him completely to serve our own desires, we can give Him just a part of ourselves, or we can give ourselves unreservedly. I know now that if you give all of yourself, you can expect almost anything—and it won't be dull.

---

[1] *Matthew* 28. 20.

Discovery at Oak Ridge

by LEN LESOURD

> ... Where atom-scientist Dr. William Pollard combines his nuclear research with a second profession—religion, which he calls "the greatest single field for future exploration and study".

WILLIAM POLLARD was a typical college graduate of 1932 —cocky, bright-eyed with ambition and convinced that man could design his own destiny.

Science, he felt, was the vehicle of sure dependable knowledge that would eventually produce the good life for all. Religion—fairy tale stuff. Pollard called himself an agnostic.

Dr. William Pollard climbed high in his profession. He helped produce the atom bomb, becoming Director of the Institute of Nuclear Studies at Oak Ridge. But if this brash 1932 graduate could have foreseen a newspaper headline about him 22 years later, he would have been stunned.

"Oak Ridge, Tennessee, 1st May 1954 . . . Dr. Pollard, physicist who helped develop the atom bomb, was ordained a priest in the Protestant Episcopal Church here today, with his four sons, ages 13–19, serving as acolytes. . . ."

What happened?

Dr. Pollard didn't abandon science for religion. He is still vitally absorbed in atomic research.

I visited Dr. Pollard in Oak Ridge. Together we went over the step-by-step process in his burial of agnosticism. It is really the story of a whole decade where men groped desperately for values and beliefs—an era of confused thinking, "isms", and misdirected energies.

Soon after graduation young Pollard got a graduate fellowship at Rice University and married attractive Marcella Hamilton. Three months after the wedding, Marcella asked him pointedly to go to a Sunday morning service with her.

"I'm sorry, Marcella, but I have more important work," he said.

Pollard went to his desk, but thought only about his wife. If his sitting through a church service would keep harmony at home, he reasoned, I'd better do it.

But he remained an agnostic and refused to say the Creed . . . "I considered it ridiculous." He did agree, however, to religious training for the children.

In 1944 Pollard went to Columbia University to do research on the gaseous-diffusion method of extracting U-235 (the explosive in atomic bombs) from common uranium. He could sense something big brewing early in World War II.

The atom bomb was exploded. Pollard and his colleagues were exhilarated. A second bomb fell on Nagasaki. Then Pollard became immersed in a whole wave of reflections as he saw the infinite potentialities of atom power. At this moment came the first grave doubts that man could, through science, control his own destiny.

At the time the Nagasaki bomb was dropped, the Pollards lived in Mt. Vernon outside New York City. That night Marcella noted something strange in her husband's attitude. After dinner, Pollard put on his coat.

"I'm going out for a while," he said.

He went to the New Rochelle Trinity Episcopal Church. Pollard admits that it was like being there for the first time. "The hymns, readings, prayers and sermon had words that now held meaning for me. The service hadn't changed, but something in me had."

After the war Dr. Pollard became executive director of the Institute of Nuclear Studies at Oak Ridge. Here was a thriving community that had sprung up around a vital new industry. Many of the buildings were hastily built. If it had been a community with established churches, the course of Pollard's life might not have changed.

Services of the local Episcopal Church were held in the high school gymnasium. One Sunday Pollard casually asked the minister about the possibilities of a real church building. Result—he was asked to head up the building fund drive. Reluctantly, he agreed. Then the Sunday School superintendent left the study for the ministry. Would Dr. Pollard take his place? How could he refuse! He had four sons going to Sunday School.

Sunday School work became so fascinating that Pollard spent many hours of study in the library so he would be able to answer the youngsters' questions. The Rector heard about Pollard's effective Sunday School talks and approached him.

"Dr. Pollard, would you be willing to become a lay reader?"

Lay reading, the Rector explained, meant reading appropriate prayers from the Book of Common Prayer at morning and evening church services. Again, somewhat hesitantly, Pollard agreed.

"Each of these steps seemed temporary," Pollard recalls. "I expected at any moment that my interest would cool or that I'd find something in religion I couldn't swallow as a scientist."

While saying their prayers, Pollard wondered about their origin. This drew him into a reading programme and a thorough study of the Bible. He found it absorbing. It was then pointed out to him that the duties of a deacon in the Episcopal church were only slightly greater than a lay reader's. A deacon can assist at Holy Communion, and if licensed by the bishop, give sermons. It meant the equivalent of three years at seminary, but Pollard was attracted by the idea of planning his religious studies as he did his scientific work. He developed a plan to do both.

"My approach was still more curious than dedicated," he admits.

To his wife, who had merely wanted him to go to church on Sunday, he tried to underplay it all by saying he could pull out at any time. Marcella must have smiled often at this casual explanation.

Meanwhile, what conflicts between scientific and theological points filled Pollard's mind?

"I expected these to occur as I approached each new phase of theology," he said. "But I found nothing in my studies that belittled the importance and need for science. Actually I began to see there should be much more to life than a desire to explain and control natural phenomena. There is man's sense of wonder and joy before the lovely mystery of the world. I could feel the deep human need for Communion with God.

"The result was I began to lay a new foundation of thinking about the universe . . . now viewed in terms of man's responsibility to God, his participation in God's purpose for the world, his response to the loving God through Christ."

Pollard made no attempt to conceal his religious interests from colleagues at the Institute. One researcher considered resigning because he felt his professional colleagues throughout the country would believe that the Institute was dominated by religious influence and would doubt the scientific value of the work.

Pollard admired this man for his blunt honesty. In a two-hour talk together they minced no words. "I have no intention of misusing my position," Pollard told him, "but I insist on the right to live my personal life as I see fit."

Both finally agreed that neither wanted the other out of the Institute. The researcher decided to stay on, collaborate with Pollard, but his felings about religion have not changed.

Pollard's five-year term as executive director of the Institute of Nuclear Studies was up in 1952. Before the board (a group of nine distinguished educators and scientists) met to consider his re-appointment, Pollard knew he had to make a personal decision. If it came to a showdown, which career was most important to him—science or religion?

Pollard, who 20 years ago would have scoffed at the use of prayer to make such a decision, now turned to it without reservations. At the meeting, he spoke his convictions frankly to members of the board.

"There's something you ought to know," he told them. "In two weeks I'll be taking my examination for ordination in the Episcopal Church. If I am ordained, I do not think it will in any way affect my direction of the Institute.

"I am aware, however, that some denomination universities among our sponsors might object. I do not want to leave the Institute, but I'll certainly understand it if you ask me to."

They asked him to leave the room. In five minutes he was called back. They had voted Pollard a new five-year term and a raise in salary.

When Pollard was ordained as full Episcopal priest in May, 1954, the transformation of an agnostic was complete. The curious attitude had become wholly dedicated.

But reporters, looking for a dramatic conversion story, were disappointed. Pollard wanted no publicity. What statements he made stressed the fact that his change was gradual and largely unforeseen. To paraphrase St. Paul, "It was not my own doing, but the gift of God, lest any man should boast."

Learn the Lessons of Spiritual Healing

A MINISTER, a doctor and a reporter—all learned and outstanding persons—are among those who examine in the following pages a subject which is being more widely discussed today than ever before: spiritual healing.

These stories have been selected and grouped together because they offer examples of the Scriptural promise *that all things are possible to him that believeth*.[1] They also bear out a basic and vital fact—that Christ is just as much with us now as He was when He walked the earth nearly 2,000 years ago. We learn that Christ does heal today (1) directly and (2) through His servants who study the laws and methods of science. We find that there seems to be no set pattern to His healings. We also come to realise that man is just beginning to understand some of the mysteries about the power to heal.

As you read these selections, you will perceive that Christ does not always heal the way we want or expect Him to. Nor should we ever forget that while Jesus healed many physical ailments, He was primarily concerned with bringing men to the Kingdom of God. Christ prepares us for the greatest victory of all—the triumph of the spirit.

Norman Vincent Peale

[1] Mark 10. 23.

A Minister Writes on the Power to Heal

by ALFRED WILLIAM PRICE

> Most doctors agree today that mental attitudes are all-important in matters of health. But can the healing miracles of the New Testament be repeated in this day and age? A well-known minister gives his answer . . .

IT was after the service had ended that I noticed the young couple waiting to see me. They had a tiny, blanket-wrapped baby with them. I still remember the look in their eyes when they told me that their child was spastic—unable to grow or develop properly. They had heard of the healing services at our church, St. Stephen's in Philadelphia. They thought or rather they hoped and prayed that if I would lay my hands on their child, the Lord might hear their prayers . . .

I took the baby from the parents and asked them to kneel at the chancel rail while I carried the baby to the altar. There, as always, I sought consecration through prayer: "O Lord, take my mind and think through it. Take my heart and set it on fire with love. Take these hands and through them bring to these, Thy suffering children, the fullness of Thy healing power. Amen."

As I prayed, the baby began to cry. She kept on crying, not just for an hour or so, but for two solid days and nights. The young parents, naturally, were frantic. They telephoned me the next day, saying that the child would not eat and could not sleep. What had happened? What *was* happening?

I tried to reassure them by telling them that, in my opinion, the marvellous process of spiritual healing had begun. I told them of other cases I had seen in which equally violent reactions had accompanied such healing. To our great joy, when the child stopped crying on the second day, a perfect cure had taken place. Today Nancy is a fine, robust little girl.

A miracle? Yes, if you consider the power of God when so manifested to be a miracle. Here at St. Stephen's we have seen it happen so often that our reaction now tends to be one of joyous, grateful acceptance, rather than shock or surprise.

It all began—for me, at least—shortly after I was called to St. Stephen's in 1942. Many people came to me with their troubles: mental, emotional, spiritual, and sometimes physical. I did my best to help them, and prayed constantly for strength and guidance. But there always seemed to be some I could not reach, could not help.

I remember one man who came to me, badly crippled with arthritis and filled with bitterness because he had been passed over for promotion in his job, a promotion he felt he deserved. I tried to make him see that he must put aside his resentment, and seek God's guidance. But I failed utterly; he went away in the same black mood of misery and despair.

I could not get this man out of my mind. I knew he was ill, both in body and spirit. And then, by coincidence perhaps, an innocent-looking little pamphlet came in the mail. It told of the success some ministers had had with the Laying-on-of-Hands Service, a part of the Episcopal ritual, for those sick in body, soul, or mind.

In the past I had used this service during Lent, or whenever some sick parishioner asked for it, but in those days the thought of having a *public* healing service seemed much too bold a step. "Could this be God's guidance?" I asked myself doubtfully. I knew that many people considered spiritual healing sensational and emotionally questionable. Then, too, there was the possibility that it might do more harm than good if results did not measure up to high hopes. But if I could be sure that this was what God wanted . . .

At last I went into the church and sat down in a front pew to pray and think this thing through. Our beautiful 134-year-old house of God had never failed to inspire me. The rich heritage that was mine came through the lives of those who had worshipped here long before I was born. If they could talk to me, I wondered, would they approve healing services?

I glanced at the many memorial plaques on the pews and then at the one where I sat. It had belonged to Dr. S. Weir Mitchell, the great neurologist and pioneer of psychosomatic medicine. For years Dr. Mitchell had been a faithful member of St. Stephen's. Surely he would approve of healing services, for he had often said, "It's not the body that is ill, but the mind."

I turned in my Bible to a passage I had read many times to my congregation: *Is any sick among you? Let him call for the elders of the church; and let them pray over him, anointing him with oil in the name of the Lord: And the prayer of faith shall save the sick, and the Lord shall raise him up; and if he has committed sins, they shall be forgiven him.*[1]

I rose from the doctor's pew strengthened, determined to follow God's leading in connection with healing services, whatever the cost might be. I knew that what I planned to do was based on Jesus' teaching. No one could deny that He was both Teacher and Physician. Jesus preached redemption of the *whole* man—body, mind, and spirit.

In our church a healing service doesn't differ much from any formal service of worship. We open with prayers and a short message on faith and health. Then I invite those who wish to kneel at the altar for the laying-on-of-hands, while I go to the altar to seek consecration through the prayer.

[1] James 5. 14, 15.

Next, I go to the chancel, and after laying my hands upon the head of each person who has come forward, I pray: "May the mercy of God and the love of our Lord Jesus Christ and the power of His Holy Spirit which are here now enter your soul, your mind and your body for healing. Amen."

Over a span of nearly 15 years I have watched these people come, not seeking an easy way out of their problems, but looking for an opportunity to grasp the true purpose of the Incarnation: *I am that they might have life, and that they might have it more abundantly.*[1]

At first, I was somewhat frightened by this power that God had allowed to flow through my hands. But as time went on, I learned to go forward with confidence in His Great Will.

Some of the cures at St. Stephen's have been swift and dramatic. A mother, with a hand swollen to three times its normal size from arthritis, received the laying-on-of-hands. She came back to church the following week, completely cured, and asked to have her now useful hand dedicated to the service of the Lord.

Not all healings happen so quickly; many come slowly over a period of months, or even years. The case of Mrs. Sadie Desabaye's son, Bobby, is an example. Bobby was born on 25th October 1945 with a club foot. His right foot was almost embedded in the leg. Mrs. Desabaye, now a widow, had great faith and courage from the start. When Bobby was 11 months old, she began to massage and try to stretch the tendons. Some progress was made, but when the baby began to try to walk, he had great difficulty.

Eventually she phoned me and asked if I thought she should bring Bobby to the healing service. I told her to do so. Bobby, then only three-and-a-half, could not kneel at the altar; so his mother knelt, holding him in her arms. I placed my hands on both their heads. Mrs. Desabaye said she had a wonderful feeling that all would be well and

[1] *John* 10. 10.

knew God would help Bobby. Each day, thereafter, she told me, she could almost see the foot and leg straighten. At the end of six months the child was completely healed. Today, Bobby has no trace of a club foot and is a happy, healthy little boy.

Over the years a Prayer Healing Fellowship has developed at St. Stephen's. The 80 members of this group, most of whom have received a first-hand demonstration of God's healing power in their own lives, engage in a daily chain of prayer for those who write and ask for help in their problems.

That the medical profession respects and commends the work is attested by the fact that the Prayer Healing Fellowship lists four doctors and several nurses among its members. These spiritually mature members prayed for 3,704 sick or troubled persons last year. Forty per cent of this number wrote that they had received complete healing or a solution to their problems.

What about the other 60 per cent? It is true that they seem to represent failure from our human point of view. But if sickness continues, we believe it is because something either in the person or in the world in which he lives is hindering God's purpose of wholeness.

In our healing ministry, our primary effort is to have the sick person healed in the area of the mind and soul. When this is accomplished, the physical healing often comes as a by-product. The Christian ideal it to have a God-filled personality, not for health's sake, but for God's sake, and for the sake of our fellow men. All the healing agencies are buried within us, waiting to be released. This is the heart of the Gospel, that the power of the Holy Spirit within us should be released to give us wholeness of life.

A Doctor Examines the Power to Heal
by OMAR JOHN FAREED, M.D.

> *Out in California a new type of clinic is trying to help people who are ill, not by dealing with isolated symptoms, but through treating the whole personality: body, mind and spirit. One of the founders of that clinic, a prominent physician, tells how it works.*

THE patient had suffered from migraine headaches for more than 20 years. A professional pharmacist, he had become frightened when 100 codeine tablets a week failed to give him relief. On the recommendation of a specialist, he came to the Fareed-Holmes Foundation.

How could we hope to succeed where others had failed?

We were dedicated to a new venture in human integration based on the theory that most people who are ill, emotionally disturbed, or unhappy can be restored only by treating the whole person—body, mind, and spirit.

The five of us—a physician, two ministers, a lawyer, and an educator (plus a consultant psychiatrist, business administrator, or other counsellors as the individual cases require)—donate one afternoon each week to these experiments. The pharmacist was one of our typical cases.

First, we gave him a thorough physical examination, confirming the findings that, other than low blood pressure which could not have caused 20 years of migraine headaches, he was physically fit.

He was administered a series of psychological tests. The patient consulted one of the ministers for spiritual evaluation. We explained to him the emotional stresses, complexes, and inhibitions lodged below the level of his conscious mind.

The real turning point came, however, when our

evaluation revealed that his spiritual needs required emphasis. From that time he spent a half hour before each panel meeting alone with either Dr. Holmes or the Reverend William Hornaday, gaining an increased understanding of affirmative prayer, actually praying with them.

The pharmacist learned this type of prayer and repeated it many times: "Dear Father, I know there is a Power in the universe greater than myself—an all-good, all-loving Power. That Power is God. As I turn to You, I know only peace, serenity and poise."

Within a few months the pharmacist was entirely freed from headaches and the need for codeine.

As the medical man involved, I could claim credit for only a small part of this result. Without doubt, the greatest therapy in this case came from affirmative prayer.

From the time when I first began in the field of medicine, I have always believed whole-heartedly in my particular science. Personally I was a materialist, although not to be confused with an agnostic nor an atheist, for I had always believed in a higher Power. Nor did I disbelieve in the power of prayer; I simply disregarded it.

My medical training had accented those things that I could dissect, measure under a microscope. I trusted that which I could analyse, measure, and test.

How, then, do I find myself today on a panel determined to establish scientifically the interrelation of physical, psychological, and spiritual factors and to test their combined healing power?

Partially, it is a legacy from my father, Ameen U. Fareed, M.D., a pioneer in psychiatry. Partially, my high regard for another pioneer, Dr. Ernest S. Holmes, a friend of father's for over 40 years, and one of the great spiritual leaders of our times. For these two men our Foundation is named.

Pioneers, to me, are men who always stay just a little ahead, who anticipate progress. My father did that all his life. In the early part of 1900 when he became a psychiatrist, it was a fledgling science and a daring speciality. Later he believed with Carl Jung that the gap between science and the spirit of man might be bridged.

Meanwhile Ernest Holmes was trying to bridge this same gap from the field of religion, teaching an exact scientific response to prayer in order to aid the process of mental and physical healing.

When, a few years ago, these pioneers invited scientists, educators, clergymen, medical men to join their tape-recorded discussions, I acted as moderator, keeping them, as I thought, on the track.

"Prove it to me," I'd insist repeatedly. "I'm a materialist."

Gradually I became intrigued, then excited. We delved into Creative Power and from whence it came; into Intuition, that faculty in man that *knows*, and knows not precisely *how* it knows; and into Immortality. As a result, I watched my father, at 71, welcome the unknown with confidence, not in a material heaven, but deeply convinced that the individual is imperishable.

The Fareed-Holmes Foundation was established in Beverley Hills, California, in 1954. Our staff is independent of any denomination or professional group, and co-operates with all. We screen and accept cases recommended by physicians, clergymen, social service agencies, as well as lay people.

One recent case, a man in his early forties, displayed definite ulcer symptoms. Hospitalisation and X-ray revealed no active ulcer. A special diet and medication seemed to have little effect.

The patient was aware of his many personality shortcomings, but he seemed unable to establish new attitudes or patterns. A close study of his religious background revealed a negative concept of prayer and a fear complex towards God.

We discovered, for example, that his prayer contained such expressions as, "God, I am an unworthy son, a miserable sinner deserving of no good thing."

Over a period of time, the repetition of these thoughts tended to create the conditions of misery and unworthiness he described. Humility before God is important, but not carried to the extreme of self-depreciation.

When affirmative prayer was brought to his awareness, he was even more sceptical at first than the pharmacist. But when he finally accepted this idea of prayer and a new concept of a loving God, his entire spiritual life underwent a startling change. The ulcer symptoms vanished almost simultaneously.

A 50-year-old matron, passing through menopause, came to us ill, nervous and depressed. A few months before she had received a special service award from a grateful community for her outstanding contributions and activities. Now her activities were at a standstill.

Medically, the estrogenic hormone treatment was indicated. But her extreme depression and despondency, we found, came from quite another cause.

Consultation revealed that ten years before her husband had been injured in an automobile accident and, while not really invalided physically, he had adopted the rôle of a parasite. As he had grown more disagreeable, his wife had become more irritated by the situation. For some time they had lived in the same house without speaking.

Psychologically, we were able to point out to her the dangers of a mind filled, as hers had become, with resentment and hostility. Medically we did inject hormones, but we could not inject new attitudes. Here again affirmative prayer was able to complete the circle of treatment, and in two months' time she was fully functional.

Since our findings here at the Foundation have so clearly indicated the power of affirmative prayer as a healing agent, I was recently moved to re-study the case of a delicate 65-year-old lady, brought to my office five years ago suffering from acute rheumatoid arthritis. She could barely walk.

"I want you to know," she told me serenely, "that your

efforts will be supported and assisted by positive prayer."

I didn't pay much attention at the time. Medically, arthritis at 65 is a major concern, and I felt I had my work cut out for me on a strictly medical plane.

This lady was a hopeful, cheerful, and obedient patient. After three months of conservative care, and three more months' observation she completely recovered.

Now, re-studying her file, I asked myself, "Is it possible that there has been no recurrence in over five years?" She is 70 now, fully active, has had no recurrence, and no medical treatment during those intervening years.

Under the microscope, in the dissecting room, it would be impossible, perhaps, to document these results. But this much I can personally say: medical problems have, in my experience, been helped by the power of affirmative prayer, far beyond what I would have been able to accomplish alone.

We have made significant strides in the areas of medicine and psychiatric treatment of the mind during the past half century. Pioneers of today are working to integrate these with the third, and possibly the most significant and enduring realm of healing, the spiritual.

A Reporter Looks at the Power to Heal

by RUTH CRANSTON

> *What happened when a trained Protestant reporter decided to investigate the spiritual healings at the great Catholic shrine of Lourdes? A firsthand report.*

Is there actually such a thing as spiritual healing? Does the hand of God sometimes reach out and miraculously set aside all the known laws of medicine? Have there really been verified cases where cancer disappeared, where blindness was cured, where broken or tubercular bones were made whole, not in weeks or months, but in minutes or seconds?

In recent years, as a Protestant reporter deeply interested in the power of faith to relieve human ills, I spent months at the famous Catholic shrine of Lourdes, exhaustively checking their carefully documented medical records. I visited Protestant centres of healing both here and abroad. I interviewed doctors of medicine and doctors of divinity. I talked to people who had received remarkable cures, and to people who had hoped and prayed for them in vain.

I had no axe to grind, nothing I wished to prove or disprove. I simply wanted to study and report the facts. And I came, ultimately, to the deep conviction that from time to time sudden healings do take place that are totally inexplicable in the light of modern knowledge.

These cures follow no set pattern. But they do happen, and careful observers have noted that they are most likely to occur when certain conditions are being met. Usually when all known medical remedies have been tried and have failed. Usually when the sufferer has reached the limits of his endurance and simply surrenders his whole being—body, mind and spirit—to a beneficent Power stronger than himself. Frequently when the person involved has lifted a burden from his heart by the confession of his own faults, or forgiveness of the faults of others. Almost always when somebody—not necessarily the sufferer himself, but *somebody* concerned—is in a state of prayer.

It is a deeply impressive thing for anyone, be he sceptic or believer, to study the system of medical checking and verification that goes on constantly at Lourdes. I was fortunate in having all the records of the Medical Bureau put at my disposal. This Bureau is composed of about 1,500 doctors and is supported by several thousand others scattered throughout the world. Some are Christians; some are Moslems; some are agnostics; some are atheists. They are all scientific, independent observers.

The Medical Bureau considers for verification only *organic* cases that are supported by carefully documented records, including before-and-after X-rays, medical examinations, and hospital files. About a hundred cases are accepted each year for examination. If the cure is tentatively verified, the patient must then present himself a year later for further review. As a rule, only about a dozen cases are ultimately certified as cures and referred to Church authorities, whose standards for acceptance are even more rigid.

Sometimes the cure is virtually instantaneous; at other times it may be spread out over a period of hours or days. But in every case, convalescence is enormously accelerated. One doctor said, "It's almost as if the capacity of the body to heal itself, or be healed instantly, were there all along, but blocked or weakened by something. With the block removed, the healing forces go into operation with speed and power."

The most remarkable experience I had while visiting Lourdes was not studying the records of physical cures, nor observing the devoted care of the sick by the well. My greatest experience was to behold the ministry of the sick to the well—and to each other.

Usually when a person falls ill of some terrible disease, he's considered finished—done for. Lourdes patients are told just the opposite. They are told that they have a tremendous work to do—for their sick brothers, for the well people around them, and for the world generally.

From the moment the ill person arrives at Lourdes, he becomes a person with a great mission. Never is he considered a human with nothing to do but wait for death. He is to serve Life—every minute of his waking hours and as long as he has breath to do it.

He is to work with the tools of the spirit. Prayer, says a

great scientist, Alexis Carrel, is the greatest power in the world. The sick still have that power. They can still pray. Not (they are taught) just for their own cure, but for the salvation and well-being of their sick comrades, and for the whole world.

I will never forget standing in the big Square in front of the sanctuaries, where the sick in the form of a great cross were praying for us, the well. All of a sudden I caught the eye of one of the sick—a young girl wasted with tuberculosis. She smiled at me. Her lips as I looked began to move, her eyes, her whole face, earnestly imploring. It would be a really hardened sinner who could do an evil thing after he had once had that experience, seen that look in a dying person's eyes—interceding, imploring for *him*.

One case of the sick's ministering to the sick had an unexpected and dramatic ending. Some three years ago Mrs. Winifred Feely arrived at Lourdes from London. She was not only sick, but dying. Her doom had been sealed by X-rays, made under the direction of some of the most eminent physicians in London, which revealed a growth between the pulmonary artery and the heart.

The doctors prescribed no treatment—simply 'rest'—and ordered her to be as quiet as she could. Mrs. Feeley suffered agonising pain, certain she was going to die. Her one desire was to go to Lourdes. Her husband had died a few years before, so she went alone, and by third-class, like most pilgrims.

She went not to ask for her cure, but to pray for a 'good' death, quiet and peaceful, and not to be a trouble to people.

At Lourdes, she took a room in a hotel. Then she went to the Hospital of the Asile and—even though so ill—offered her services. She knew Lourdes. She asked if she could take the ambulatory patients about—showing them the Sanctuaries, the museums, Bernadette's home, and so on. The Sister told her to come back at two o'clock. By that time there was an amazing group ready to accompany her, the shaking palsied ones, the cripples—the lame, the halt, and the blind, literally. For two hours she trailed around with them.

But their guide, after this exhausting afternoon, had a desperate night. Now, she thought, I am really dying. Next day she did not want to go to the baths, but did—as a sort of penance—because it was a hard thing to do.

After the bath, she sat there in the cramped dressing-room, head bent over, feeling terrible, but even then scolding herself. "Stop it! Stop thinking about yourself. *Pray*. See what you can do for other people. Try to help somebody else."

She heard someone call her. "Madame, could you please help me to lift this lady?" One of the nurses was asking her to help lift a woman on to a stretcher. She went over and did it. Afterwards she said to herself, "Why, *you* can't do that; it nearly kills you to lift a water pitcher."

Another voice called, "Madame, would you please help me to put on my stockings?" A great fat peasant woman, purple in the face, looking up to her beseechingly. A poor woman—smelly, unattractive. Probably like the people whose feet Jesus washed.

She helped her put on the stockings—bending over.

Suddenly she tried raising her arm over her head—the movement that usually gave her exquisite agony. She could do it perfectly well. It then began to dawn on her what had happened. "No! No, it can't be—not to me. Not to me!"

She turned and ran out of the bath-house—ran, fairly flew to the Grotto. Knelt down and made her thanksgiving. She wanted to go to Mass, found it was being held high up in the Basilica. Again she *ran* up those 170 steep steps.

Afterwards, coming down, she met one of the Medical Bureau doctors who knew all about her. He gazed at her, astounded. Then a big smile spread over his face. "Well, Mrs. Feely," he said softly, "Our Lady has been very good to you!"

"It was the sick," she said, between laughing and crying. "The sick, bless them, called out, and Our Lady heard!"

Winifred Feely has never known a sick day since that moment. Her X-ray, before and after, are the most impressive confirmation of the story. She is still at Lourdes, doing volunteer work among the sick.

How shall we explain these sudden and dramatic instances of healing without medical intervention? Materialists may seek an explanation in some form of auto-suggestion. I prefer to agree with Father John LaFarge. "For those who believe in God," he said, "no explanation is necessary. For those who do not believe in God, no explanation is possible."

I Saw It Happen

by IVAN H. HAGEDORN

When doctors could not restore Naomi's failing eyesight, she sought a cure through spiritual means. The climax came at an Easter Service.

As I stood in the vestry watching the congregation entering my church last Easter morning, I could sense a feeling of expectancy in the air. A sixteen-year-old girl, with a dark patch covering her eye, entered with her mother and quietly took her place in the pew.

The girl was Naomi Irene Crowley. Because of failing eyesight, she had been coming to me for pastoral advice.

While gazing out over the congregation, I had a swift feeling of inadequacy that comes occasionally to a minister. Naomi and those close to her hoped and prayed for a healing. God answers our prayers, but not always the way we want Him to.

Naomi's difficulty had begun many months ago, but she

had continued her high school activities. Eventually, fading vision could no longer be ignored, and in November of 1952, an operation was performed to restore the vision in her right eye and to straighten the slant in her left eye.

For a time it seemed as though the operation was successful. Then, in January, 1953, Naomi became totally blind. Specialists were called and, after careful examinations, they undertook a second operation.

Naomi lay in the hospital for a month. The adjoining bed was occupied by a negro woman, Mrs. John Carter, and one day, as Naomi lay in darkness, the kindly woman said, "Naomi, there's a motto on the wall of this room, and it says 'The Lord is my Shepherd. I shall not want.'"

Then Mrs. Carter would take her hand to confidently assure her, "You'll be all right, honey. You'll be all right. The Lord says He is your Shepherd and you shall not want —not even for your vision."

At last Naomi was sent home. The operation had been only partially successful; while the sight in one eye was restored, the other eye was completely blind.

For two months after returning home, Naomi was required to wear a black patch over her eye. An attractive girl, she found this a hardship. One day, as she was returning home with a package of groceries, a little boy, with the thoughtless cruelty of the young, tugged at her arm and said, "You know what? You look like a pirate?"

Despite such incidents which caused her secret grief Naomi found most people treated her very kindly. Hearing of her story, an interested priest asked, "May I bless your eyes?" Naomi agreed.

At the Philadelphia high school she attended, classmates of all faiths offered prayers in her behalf.

One day she met a friend who suggested, "Naomi, why don't you go to some faith-healing sect?" The next evening she visited me to ask, "Pastor, what do you think?"

"Naomi, you are a Christian girl," I answered after some reflection, "and I am sure that God will as readily hear our prayers, yours and mine, as any others which might be addressed to Him." Naomi agreed and, before she left, we prayed together.

Never throughout this trying time did Naomi give up the belief that God would answer her prayers by restoring her sight. But often I worried at what would happen to her faith if the response were not as she expected.

On Easter morning, Naomi rose early. Later she told me, "I did not plan to go to the Sunrise Service. However, something far stronger than myself insisted. It just seemed as though something said, "Go! God, on the day of His resurrection, will remember you . . . !"

Easter morning was bright and beautiful. The church overflowed with people. Many, unable to squeeze into the auditorium, stayed in adjoining rooms to which the service was carried by amplifiers. The rough-hewn cross that had been erected in the chancel, and which had stood gaunt and naked over Holy Thursday and Good Friday, was now covered with beautiful flowers.

As the service began, I greeted the congregation with the stirring words, "The Lord is risen."

The response came, "He is risen, indeed."

The service proceeded in all its inspiring beauty. Then, finally, it was over and the recessional hymn swelled out over the auditorium.

Suddenly Naomi began to sway dizzily. Her mother helped her to sit down, but Naomi fainted. During the commotion the patch fell from her eye. In a few moments Naomi began to revive. Slowly she blinked.

"Mother!" she exclaimed. "I can see. I *can* see."

And then, beyond her mother's radiant face, the Cross garlanded with dogwood seemed to fill Naomi's horizon. "And oh, the Cross, it is so beautiful!"

For a moment, the circle of people around Naomi stood in confusion. Then, as each turned to his neighbour and spoke of the healing, a low murmur of voices filled the auditorium, swelled and ebbed to an awed silence.

Then, from the rear of the church came a hushed whisper, "He is risen." One by one, other voices joined the whisper and the words gained power and strength. And then, like a giant wave, the chant rolled forward as the entire congregation repeated over and over, "He is risen. He is risen, indeed."

Opportunity in Work Clothes

by HENRY J. KAISER, JR.

From the family of master builders comes a vital blueprint: on how to face a personal handicap.

ONE night during World War II, I was working late at our Fontana, California steel plant. Around midnight the phone rang. It was Father calling from New York.

"Didn't you build model planes as a kid?" he asked crisply.

"I sure did."

"Good," he said. "Can you fly here tomorrow?"

"Certainly, but what's it all about?"

"The Navy wants us to build fighter planes. You probably know as much about this as anyone else here does. What time will you arrive?"

When I hung up, I was frightened. But not too frightened to take on a job which might seem over my head. And we did turn out the planes, exceeding the production schedule. Believe me, I had fun working on this project—an exciting experience I'll never forget.

Many engineers in this country thought it would be impossible to build the great Bonneville Dam. My father had the vision and faith that it could be done. Against the advice of the bonding companies, who refused to bond him, he undertook the job.

How did he do it? He put my brother, Edgar, a young man, in charge, then gathered together other key young men to help him. My father's associates were aghast. "You can't let 'boys' handle such a project," they said.

The 'boys' went ahead and completed the job. Afterwards one of the top Army engineers summed up the project to my father with the terse comment: "The kids succeeded because they never had been licked. They didn't know it couldn't be done."

Now there's nothing 'hit-or-miss' about my father's building techniques. Many a time I've heard him say, "When a man builds, he does not start with cement or stone or steel. He starts with a basic principle." There must be a blueprint—a central plan.

From the time I was a youngster, Dad always brought his business home and discussed it with the family. We were all very much a part of it, and in our closeness to each other shared everything together. We were captured by the excitement of big projects; our imaginations were constantly soaring.

Nor have I known a more deeply religious man than my father. Although he didn't talk much about it, the spirit of his faith permeated everything he did. It conditioned him —and his family—mentally, to shrug off defeats and mistakes and go on to the next bigger thing.

"A problem is an opportunity in work clothes," my father often said.

I liked this motto—and had good cause to remember it and use it at the end of World War II.

At the time I was in charge of our Denver and Fontana shell plants and was constantly on the go. In three months I lost 50 pounds.

One day in Denver while hurrying down the hall to my office, my legs buckled under me as though they had turned to rubber. I couldn't walk. Dazed, I was carried to a doctor for an examination.

"You have multiple sclerosis," he said. "There is little

we can do for you, except advise you to rest and hope that it doesn't get worse."

For one so active it was like a sentence to a living death. Waves of self-pity and discouragement swept over me. Mechanically, I allowed myself to be led from doctor to doctor. Eventually, we visited Dr. Herman Kabat, in Washington, D.C.

"Henry, I think I can help you," said Dr. Kabat. "We'll have to use some of the excess nerve capacity of your body to re-train those muscles. It depends on how much hard work you're willing to put forth."

At the time it seemed to me like telling a man he could lift a mountain if he had the determination. Then it occurred to me, "Perhaps an illness can be an opportunity in work clothes."

I got down to work. For hours each day I exercised. After a few weeks I was able to move my toes for the first time since my collapse.

Meanwhile, I had been doing some thinking. You cannot construct a building without a basic plan, I reasoned. So if I were to build a new life, a blueprint was needed. Furthermore, I knew that such a plan would have to start with God.

In my prayers I said something like this: "God, I'll do everything I can physically about this disease. If You give me the strength, I'll know it's up to me to put it to work. More than anything else, I want to walk again and get back on the job. But if it doesn't work out that way, then I'll find something else to do. Please give me the tools You want me to use."

My wife, Bobbie, bless her, has helped me in a thousand ways. Her patience and faith have deepened my own belief. Together we have learned much about prayer.

Over a period of time I did get back on my feet and gradually was able to resume my duties at the office.

Several years ago we built a new home amidst the towering pines on the hilltop overlooking the San Francisco-

Oakland bay area. Both our blueprint for this home and for a more effective life were woven together in the form of a prayer garden.

Bobbie and I use it daily, to seek strength and guidance, to thank God for the fact that I can resume my activities. The garden is a beautiful spot. At the back of the altar are some azaleas, two 12-foot camellias and three huge pine trees forming a perfect trinity. Green plants and shrubs form a border around the garden and lawn. The prayer garden is no substitute for church; it is an additional 'plus' in our growing religious experience.

It is hard to describe how much this spot means to us. From the quiet smile of happiness on my father's face when he first saw our garden, I could tell he understood.

Several years ago on Youth Sunday, I was invited to speak at the Church of the Holy Faith (Episcopal) in Inglewood, California. Two days before this, my father called to say he was filling the pulpit of a New York church on the same Sunday. We didn't mention our subjects, although I did ask him to send me a copy of his address.

When it arrived, I was amazed to find that the sermons we gave 3,000 miles apart that Sunday had been almost identical. On further thought I realised it was perfectly natural for both Dad and me to share, that Sunday, the spiritual principles that had made our lives an adventure.

After all, they are the most important things we have to talk about.

Know How to Forgive Others and Yourself

MANY people are handicapped in their efforts to unlock their faith-power because they will not or cannot practise forgiveness.

Do you realise what a drain it is on the mental and physical person to bear a grudge? Hannah Moore said that "Forgiveness saves the expense of anger, the cost of hatred, the waste of spirits." That these things are expensive is borne out today by a noted physician in New York who stated that some of his patients actually suffered physically from the resentments they bore. "Forgiveness will do more towards getting them better than any pills or injections," he said.

Another doctor told me one time of a man who died of what he called 'grudgitis'—a long-held hatred of another. That man might very well have profited from a reading of any one of the stories in this group, which deal with the deepest and most fragile of emotions, and which echo the words *Father, forgive them for they know not what they do*.

I have also seen many people who found it impossible to forgive themselves for a wrongdoing or a mistake. Psychiatrists call it 'self-censuring'. We must learn to forgive ourselves, even as God forgives us, if we are to achieve normal and happy lives.

Norman Vincent Peale

My Father Held the Gun

by MILTON J. COHEN

Hatred was his goad and vengeance his goal. But when the long-awaited moment came . . . something unexpected happened.

NUMBLY, I knelt beside the small, gentle man who had been my father.

"Who did it?" I choked. "In the name of God who did it?"

"Two kids. About sixteen,"' one of the patrolmen said gruffly. "That's all he had time to tell us."

I stood up, my mind and body on fire. This wasn't real, I told myself. It couldn't be real. Samuel Cohen was not lying behind the counter of his little Bronx grocery store, his stomach ripped with bullets, his cash register rifled. This was a nightmare from another world.

Then big, stolid plain-clothesmen were everywhere; questioning me and my sister Beatrice, who had been the first person in the store after it happened; going over the store for fingerprints; methodically checking the cash register; questioning possible witnesses in near-by stores and apartments. Their grim purposefulness restored me to reality. My father had been murdered by two teenage thugs for the contents of his cash register: a pitiful $6.50.

That was when the hatred began.

I was like a drunken man, talking to my wife, Lucille, that night.

"I'm going to be a cop," I said. "I'm going tomorrow. I'll find them and kill them. I won't sleep until I see them dead."

By strange coincidence, I had taken the examination for New York City patrolman two years before and placed well up on the list. My father advised me to do it, "to have something to fall back on." I had turned down an appointment the following year, deciding to finish my studies at Manhattan College and go on to a career in accounting. But I knew I could be put back on the list if I requested it.

Lucille reasoned me out of this headlong decision and convinced me that I should at least complete my college courses. But no one on earth could reason me out of my hatred. It went with me when I returned to school, a cold, grim hunger. I sat in class and listened to my teachers, Christian Brothers, who were giving their lives to bring young men to wisdom. I respected and admired these dedicated men. But my hatred remained.

Night after night I haunted the 50th Precinct, not far from my home, waited in vain for the killers to be caught. Finally one hard-eyed detective told me the case was almost hopeless; there was no on-the-spot witnesses, no worth-while descriptions.

That night I said to Lucille: "I'm going back on the list. I'll be appointed right after I graduate."

Lucille's eyes dropped. She knew exactly what was wrong. But she didn't argue with me. "If that's what you want, Milton . . ."

To understand my hunger for vengeance, you have to know something about my father. If there were saints in our Jewish religion, he would be one. He did not drink or smoke or gamble. He lived for other people—his children and his friends.

My mother died when I was seven. My father raised me and three older sisters alone. Though he was deeply educated in his own religion, he was pleased when I chose Manhattan for my college, because he wanted me to understand and respect other faiths. He welcomed my Protestant wife into the family as if she were his own daughter.

For twenty-three years he had owned and operated the small grocery on 238th Street off Broadway. He was an institution in the neighbourhood. Everybody loved him: kids in search of something sweet; families to whom he gave endless credit during hard times; clergymen of all faiths, to whom he was always making donations. On his bier were hundreds of Mass cards and letters of sympathy from Catholics and Protestants.

I graduated from college on 9th June 1953. On 16th June I was sworn in as a patrolman. The cold hunger was still inside me. I was going to get even the first chance I got. It wouldn't have to be my father's killers. I knew it was absurd to hope to find them now. Any thug would do.

For the first 12 months I was the most disappointed policeman in New York. I was assigned to the West 30th Street Precinct, in the heart of the garment district. It was routine duty.

Then the Precinct began sending two men on 'fly duty' each night to the West 100th Street Station, an area with the highest crime rate in the city. I volunteered to go every night, though it meant working from 6.00 p.m. to 2.00 a.m.

On Friday, 13th August 1954, I was patrolling on Morningside Drive near 118th Street; it was 1.45 in the morning, a quiet night so far. Suddenly, up ahead at the corner, there was a tremendous crash and then pistol shots. I pulled my gun and started running.

I got to the corner just in time to see Patrolman Arthur Reilly chasing a man down Morningside Drive. Another, younger, thug was legging it for all he was worth in the other direction, towards 118th Street. I took off after him.

He had a good block headstart on me, but he didn't know I was chasing him. He had seen only Reilly, whom he knew had gone in the other direction after his partner. He stopped on the corner of Morningside Drive and 119th Street to look back and see what was happening. In ten seconds I was on top of him, my gun out.

I had waited twenty-one months for this moment.

He had his knife in his hand, ready for use. There wasn't a reason in the world why I shouldn't shoot him.

My gun came up. My finger tightened on the trigger, tightened by the blind hate in me. He was young. He might even be the killer I wanted . . . but I couldn't press the trigger.

Why? Why? Why?

Because my father wouldn't let me. He could not hate.

Then he spoke to me. In all those months since his murder, I had lived in a blind fury of hatred, never thinking of him as speaking, only thinking of him as gone, as lost for ever.

But in that instant, I realised he wasn't lost. He was alive, within me. His hand was on this gun as much as mine. And his finger would never pull the trigger, even if this were his killer before me.

Slowly, my fingers eased off. One swing of my nightstick and the young thug's knife clattered to the pavement. I marched him back down Morningside Drive, where I found Reilly waiting with his man. A little farther up the street was a wrecked taxicab, the driver slumped in the front seat bleeding from stab wounds in the neck and throat.

We took the driver to the station, gave him first aid and booked his two would-be robbers.

Lucille was waiting up for me, as usual, when I came in. I told her what had happened. Then, together, we went in and looked down at our sleeping babies, Billy, 3, and Sherry, 5 months.

"I feel free," I said. "For the first time in a long while."

"You are," Lucille said softly. "Free to be the kind of a father your father was."

A Pickpocket Faces Tomorrow

A Guideposts' editor travelled to a distant city to verify this story. The author is in his late fifties. He is trying to start life anew, to leave behind him his record of crime and indolence. We do not know whether he will win his fight. We pray that he does and hope that your prayers go with him.

As a kid, I dreamed of high adventure—of travel and intrigue, of danger and fortune.

At 16, with my heart set upon being a jockey, I wangled a reluctant permission from my parents to work for a racing stable. From that time on I roamed the country, taking care of myself alone, never understanding the meaning of, nor the reason for, honest productivity.

I never got to be a full-fledged jockey because I found the easy way to quick money first. In a hotel where I mingled with gamblers and other fast-money fellows, I met a group of men who were pickpockets. One man in particular, Danny, I asked to teach me his trade. Danny blew up.

"What do you think I am, a Fagin?" he shouted. "Go home, boy, and don't come near us again!" With a hard boot he kicked me out.

The next day another pickpocket, who laughed when I told him about Danny, said, "I'll teach you, kid, if you'd like to join up with me. One of my 'stalls' has left town, and I can use you."

That was how I joined the 'light-fingered fraternity'—as a 'stall', the accomplice who distracts the 'mark' or prospective victim.

And a fraternity it is. Pickpockets—'cannons', 'dips', 'light-fingers', or 'whizzes', as they are known—have a world of their own and don't mix much with people outside their profession. They have their code of honour—not to ply their trade in bars, looking for over-loaded drinkers; not to prey upon the fairer sex (those who do so are purse-snatchers and are not recognised by professionals). They have reunions, in city after city, for they are gypsies, always on the move.

Very few pickpockets operate alone—it's too difficult—but nothing is impossible for a really good whizz. No pocket is safe from him; no safety clasp will secure a stud or stick-pin from his reach. He can remove a man's braces without the wearer's feeling anything but loss of support. His eyes are alert and busy like a forest animal's, ferreting out 'marks', always on guard for plain-clothes men. Truly, the eyes are the mirror of the soul; no pickpocket will ever look straight at a member of the law.

Off and on for almost 40 years I made my living by picking pockets, stealing. I spent three terms in prison. There were times when I tried to go straight. Once, when I fell in love, I became a bellhop, but the break-up of the romance sent me scurrying back to 'the boys'. Another time, fresh from prison, I tried selling radios. I just couldn't make a go of it. Looking back, it seems strange because I was accustomed to living by my wits, and people have always seemed to like me. Probably deep down I didn't want to succeed. I have always tried to avoid responsibility, especially when there is much work involved.

And too, pocket-picking, with its lure of fast and easy money and its covert excitement, was my disease—as alcohol is to others. Sometimes I had no idea of stealing at all, and then I'd notice a man 'fanning' his pocket (patting it frequently to make sure the contents were safe). The challenge would be too great to decline. I'd wait for the mark to remove his hand, and in a split second, I'd have his wallet. Then I'd step back and watch his reaction. I don't know whether I'd do this sort of thing because I was devilish or whether I wanted to satisfy my ego. But I did it.

About 15 years ago, my life began imperceptibly to take a different turn. One person who influenced me was a lovely widow lady, who is still my friend and a loyal one. She was always sending get-well cards and remembering people's birthdays, and walking blocks to feed pigeons.

On Sundays I'd wait for her outside church. Occasionally she would say it would be nicer if I went in with her, but she didn't press me. She said she prayed for me.

Eight years ago I travelled 1,500 miles to be with my dying father. As he struggled hard for life, I tried desperately to find new doctors, a drug, or something that could help him. There was nothing to be done. And then suddenly, as I sat beside his bed, I leaned over to my father and whispered:

"Try God. Ask God," I said. I don't know why I did it, but Dad looked at me for a long time, then folded his hands, and it seemed as though his pain eased. He died a few hours later.

At his funeral the church seemed foreign to me. Watching the altar boys—serving as I had served once—listening to the service, I felt confused. In a day I was on my way again.

A few years later I got a call, much delayed because I couldn't be located; now my mother was on the critical list. I arrived too late. Too late even for the funeral. I went to the cemetery alone and just sat there, thinking. I began to see then, for the first time, that I was a thief and a sneak and a felon; I was opposed to the rightness and goodness of life.

The years were passing and, like so many leaves falling from the trees, my friends were passing with them. The old fraternity was getting smaller. Every time I heard of another boy's going, I felt a peculiar squeamishness in me, a guilt for both our pasts, his and mine.

A couple of years later and another call from home. My sister, dangerously ill, had to have an operation. I knew it —I was losing my sister, too. The surgeon met me outside her door, saying her recovery was in the hands of a higher power than his. Then he led me in. She was lying in bed clasping a rosary, with holy medals pinned on her gown.

"It was inconsiderate of me," she said, "taking you away from your work. But I wanted to see you. I wanted to tell you that I'm going to be all right. And I wanted your help."

She gave me a prayer to St. Anthony and medals, and she asked me to pray for her.

And I did. It was hard. I no longer knew how. But I prayed. And my sister grew well.

I have not stopped praying since then. But I reserved for myself the right to make a living, and that by the only way I knew. I made a compromise with God, I thought, by giving a percentage of my 'profits' to the needy. I was too much the 'con man' to know that you don't make deals with God.

From that time on, mysterious, inexplicable things started happening. I seemed to be losing my touch. Frequently, just as I placed my fingers on a large roll of currency, it would slip from my grip. Or I'd get a wallet, and it would contain little or no money. I'd bet on a horse —I'm a fair gambler—but I'd lose.

I'd get back to my lodgings and find a letter from my sister beginning "Jesus, Mary, and Joseph" and telling me that she was praying for me. I'd see the widow, and she'd tell me she had stopped at a church to pray for me. This continued, and I was making no money. I began to blame those two women and almost curse their prayers. They were praying me out of business!

Desperate, I wandered into crowds full of detectives, something no smart pickpocket would ever do. Suddenly I would think I heard a soft voice behind me, and when I'd turn to look, I'd spot some detectives before they spotted me, and I'd be able to walk away. It was as though some strange power were guiding me.

Then, one day I lifted a fat wallet. When I opened it, I was stunned. There in my hand was the most beautiful picture of Christ I had ever seen. His arms were outstretched, and His face was full of mercy and compassion. I looked at it unbelievingly, and I started to mumble, over and over:

"Jesus, have mercy on me a sinner!"

I went to my room, and for the first time, I felt it all—the worthlessness of my life, the pain I had caused others. There in the quiet I prayed aloud:

"O God, let Thy will be done, not mine. Make me a better man. Give me strength to follow Thy guidance. Let me be Thy humble servant and serve Thee well."

When I got up, my first act was to post that wallet with its contents back to its owner.

That was one month before the end of 1954. The Christmas season, with its enormous temptations, came and went. I did not steal. I have not stolen since.

Today, I am still looking for work, living off borrowed money. It is not easy for a man my age with a long prison record and no gainful work behind him. I cannot be in crowds without the police picking me up and taking me off to a line-up of suspected criminals. It will take time for them to understand, if ever they do.

I am praying for work. I am not looking for sympathy or charity. And I write this now because I feel I must, because I want to tell people the power of prayer, and because I want to be forgiven. I know that this is possible because Jesus forgave Dismas, the thief on the cross.

The Boy Who Couldn't Face His Friends

by CLIFF MILNOR

A boy ... a loaded gun ... a tragedy. Could you have forgiven him?

THE boy had taken his father's automatic pistol without permission and, while playing with it, accidentally killed a nine-year-old girl. Residents of his rural community were grief-stricken. Most devastated of all was the boy himself.

He was 13, old enough to realise the extent of the catastrophe. By law, he had committed a crime, although he was too young to pay for it.

The boy had taken the pistol and joined several children playing in the barn behind his home. He chose a target and emptied the pistol's clip into it. Teasingly, he decided to frighten the smaller girls who had watched him. He whirled on young Marie Mills, a neighbour, and fired.

Two hours later she died in a Fort Wayne hospital. The boy had forgotten the one shell still in the chamber.

In the past, he had often eyed the pistol with curiosity; he had been admonished repeatedly by his parents to let it alone. Now his disobedience would haunt him for ever.

Marie's brother, the Reverend Sherman W. Mills, hurried home from his South Dakota church. After the funeral the Mills family gave some thought to the remorse-stricken lad.

The boy had dreaded returning to his classes, and the censure and accusation of his friends. Therefore, he was stunned when, early one morning, he saw Marie's mother and brother stop at his house to drive him to school. Arriving, the boy went to his classroom. The Reverend Mr. Mills went to the school principal. In a few moments, the student body of 570 pupils was summoned to the gymnasium.

The clergyman did not speak until they all sat silent before him.

"You all know the details," he said softly. "There's no need to go into them further. All we can hope is that my sister's death will be a lesson to all of us to be careful, in the future, whatever we're doing."

The students watched the minister intently.

"I have asked you here," he continued, "to tell you that my mother and the rest of our family have forgiven this boy for what happened. And we have asked God to forgive him, too. Furthermore, we want all of you to forgive him, and I ask you never to discuss this incident, either with him or among yourselves. His deed was not intentional, and any one of us could have been guilty of it."

The minister waited, then spoke the boy's name and asked him to come forward. The youngster stood, hesitantly. His face was pale. Nervously he wet his lips.

When the youngster reached his side, Mr. Mills warmly put his arm around the boy's shoulders. "Last night," the minister said, "my family and this boy's family gathered together for Holy Communion. We prayed that God would put charity and understanding in our hearts, so that we might love this boy during this most lonely and desperate hour of his life. Our prayer has been answered. I ask all of you to join me now in the same prayer."

His arm still around the boy, the minister whispered a plea for Divine Guidance for the students, as it had been granted to him.

Then the students rose and silently filed out. The young faces were solemn with an understanding of this majestic experience. They had learned what it meant to forgive.

This Could Happen to You
by CATHERINE CLARK

Even as you read this, police cars are racing and ambulances screaming toward the scene of another highway accident. How do you forgive a highway murderer?

OUR new car was like a dream come true. My husband and I had planned on it for so long. Like two kids with a Christmas toy, we inspected every detail—trying out the windscreen wipers, tuning in the radio, opening the glove compartment.

The dream car arrived while my sister and her family were spending a few days of their vacation with us. Although expecting my second baby and warned to keep my activities to a minimum, I decided, impulsively, to go with my sister to her Texas home. The following week-end, Clark (everyone calls him by his last name) was to drive down and pick me up in our new car.

I shall never forget how my husband looked, when we drove away, as he turned and waved good-bye.

During the five wonderful years of our marriage, we had a pet habit of silently forming the words, "I love you," with our lips. It was a little secret game we played over the heads of our friends at parties or wherever we might be. The one who said it first won the game for that time.

Now, as Clark turned and waved, he beat me at our game.

My week's visit at my sister's home was darkened by a strange fear I could not explain. I was glad when the week-end arrived and I looked forward to my husband.

On Friday night, we sat on my sister's front lawn, waiting. Hours passed. I grew nervously impatient and my eyes were glued to the direction I knew our car would approach—but it never came. At midnight, feeling some business must have detained him, we all went to bed. I stretched out fully dressed and finally fell asleep.

The piercing ring of the telephone woke me at five.

"Long distance is calling . . ." During the moments that followed tears and words were mixed together; facts jumbled. Then we threw suitcases into my sister's car, and to the steady drone of wheels I tried to piece the story together.

A head-on collision at early dusk. Two killed. Four seriously injured. Some of these might not live—one not more than two hours at the most. *And that one was my husband!*

The doctors did not want me to see my husband, but they could not stop me. They warned me about my pregnancy, but I ignored them and entered Clark's room.

I looked at him once, then kept staring at his ring. It was the only way I could recognise him, he was so smashed up. Then I reached out to him, but the nurse held me back.

"You mustn't touch him. The pain will be too much."

I sank slowly into my chair, suddenly realising that there had been others in the accident. Where were they? How badly were they hurt? Did they look like this? And what about the driver of the other car?

Later I learned about him. My husband and friends had been at a business conference, and returning home in the evening twilight hour they rounded a curve in the highway and saw a car bearing down, on the wrong side of the road.

A man had driven too far. A good man, but a tired one. He had fallen asleep at the wheel.

I wanted to hate him. I wanted to rush to him and demand: "Do you know what you've done to us—to all of us? Do you know you've killed two people? Why didn't you stop when you knew you were so tired?"

Yet something kept reminding me of my own life: the

times we had hurried, the times we were tired on the road when, by the grace of God, we escaped being the *guilty one*. We had always been lucky. None of us were bad people, just thoughtless people—sure of our driving, sure of our cars, sure of everything . . . until we were struck down.

The painful days ebbed away. My mother-in-law and I had taken a room in the near-by home of a minister and his wife. They were wonderful people, and though we were of different faiths, I knew he was praying for my husband.

One afternoon Clark suddenly took a turn for the worse. It was evident that he was dying. His mother and I faced each other across his bed. I asked her if she wanted me to get a minister and she said yes.

I hurried down the street to the minister we knew and, in silence, the two of us ran back to the hospital. Quietly he took my husband's hand and knelt beside his bed.

Something then happened in that small hospital room which is beyond understanding. Although the door was closed, it seemed suddenly that light was coming through it. The brightness pierced my closed eyes so strongly that I opened them and looked around, sensing the nearness of someone else in the room. I stepped to Clark and took his hand. It was growing warmer.

The door burst open and the doctor rushed in. Even as he worked over my husband, he said he had a fighting chance again. But I felt I had already been told that . . .

We are home now and my husband is well. I never met the man who caused the accident, but I think of him often. Not with bitterness, for I am too grateful that, despite our great physical, emotional and financial adjustments, once again my husband and I can sit in crowded rooms and play our secret game of 'I love you'.

Feeling a personal responsibility to do something about the heartaches from traffic accidents that paralyse new families every day, I sat down alone at my desk one night, two years ago, and from my heart composed a 'Driver's

Prayer'. People who take God with them behind the wheel of their car—who pray about their driving—can't help being keenly aware that they are, in truth, 'their brother's keeper'.

> Dear Lord—before I take my place
>   Today behind the wheel,
> Please let me come with humble heart
>   Before Thy throne to kneel—
>
> And pray, that I am fit to drive
>   Each busy thoroughfare,
> And that I keep a watchful eye
>   Lest some small child be there.
>
> And keep me thinking constantly
>   About the Golden Rule.
> When driving past the playground zones
>   Or by some busy school
>
> Then, when I stop to give someone
>   His right to cross the street,
> Let me—my brother's keeper be
>   And spare a life that's sweet.
>
> Please make me feel this car I drive
>   You gave me to enjoy,
> And that it's purpose is to serve
>   Mankind—but not destroy.

The above prayer copyrighted by Catherine Clark.

Change Your Life Through Prayer

A SHORT simple plea repeated over and over, urgent as an S O S. . . .

An eloquently stated request for forgiveness . . .

A thanksgiving . . .

These are the prayers about which you are now going to read. Every individual has a different way of expressing himself to God. Still it is possible that something you read here will help you with your own prayers.

The very fact that you want to pray effectively reveals to God your determination. Development in prayer requires imagination and concentration. Prayer, to be vital, must not be negative. Try picturing yourself in direct communication with God and believing that He is listening and loving you as you talk. But most of all, know that God really answers your prayers. Maybe He doesn't always answer them the way we want Him to, but then, His blessings often come disguised. I have learned that God answers our prayers in three ways: either with *yes, no* or *wait*. But answer them He always does.

Norman Vincent Peale

God, Send Someone!

by DICK SULLIVAN

A cave-in. A man buried alive. A desperate prayer for help. This is the amazing documentation of how that prayer was answered.

At 4.00 p.m. on 14th June 1955, my brother Jack Sullivan was just crawling down into a ten-foot-deep trench which ran down the centre of Washington Street, a main thoroughfare in West Roxbury, Massachusetts.

It was near quitting time. Jack is a welder, and he wanted to finish one particular part of his job before he left. Jack said good-bye to the other men as they quit, took his welding lead in his right hand, lowered himself and his electric power cable into the trench. His head was below street surface.

It was Jack's job to weld the joints of a new water main both inside and out. First Jack crawled into the 36-inch-diameter pipe, lowered his mask to protect his eyes against the bright welding arc, then went to work. After completing the inside of the joint he crawled out of the pipe. It was 4.30 p.m. He began to weld the outside. Halfway through he stood up to get the kinks out of his legs. Jack stretched, pulled down the shield again. And then it happened.

The bank caved in. Tons of dirt came crushing down on him from above and behind.

Jack was rammed against the pipe with the force of a sledge hammer. He went down, buried in a kneeling position; his shield slammed against the pipe; his nose flattened out against the inside of the shield.

The pain started. He felt his shoulder burning against the red-hot section of pipe he had been welding. He tried to move the shoulder back from the pipe. He couldn't.

His nose began to pain him. It was bleeding.

Jack tried calling. Three times he shouted. The sound of his voice died in his shield. He tried to breathe slowly to preserve the supply of oxygen.

It crossed Jack's mind that he might die.

Slowly he began to pray. Going to Mass at St. Patrick's once a week suddenly seemed quite inadequate. My brother continued to pray. He had his eyes open. It was black.

Something cool crossed his right hand. He wiggled his fingers. They moved freely. His right hand had not been buried. He moved the hand again. He tried to scratch around with his hand to open up an air passage down his arm. But the weight of the earth was too great. It didn't do any good.

Then it occurred to him that he'd been holding the welding lead in that hand. So he fished around with his fingers. He found the rod, still in the holder. He grasped it tightly and moved it, hoping it would strike the pipe. Suddenly his wrist jerked and he knew he had struck an arc —the electric current would be making its bright orange flash. So he kept on tapping on the pipe, making an arc, hoping it would draw attention.

"That must look like something," Jack thought to himself. "A hand reaching out of the ground striking an arc against the pipe. That must really look like something."

He began to figure how long he'd been buried. Of course there was no way of telling time. He wondered how much petrol was left in the engine-driven welder up on top of the trench—whether it would last until dark when the orange arc might draw attention. Then he remembered that it was almost the longest day in the year; darkness wouldn't fall until nearly nine o'clock.

He thought of all the hundreds of people passing within feet of him up above . . .

He thought of his family and wondered if he'd ever see his litttle grandson again . . .

He thought of Tommy Whittaker, his assistant, out on another job on Route 128 . . .

He figured there wasn't anything to do but lie there and wait and keep tapping flashes, and hope enough air filtered into the mask. There wasn't anything to do but lie there and pray . . . God, send someone . . . someone . . .

In another part of Boston, out on Route 128, Jack's assistant, Tommy Whittaker, quit his work for the day. Whittaker is 47 years old. Jack is 41. They had known each other for over 15 years and were close friends.

Tommy Whittaker did not know that Jack was on the Washington Street job. Whittaker got in his truck and started off down Route 128 with the full intention of driving directly home. Route 128 is a main artery, a super highway that could take him home within minutes.

But as Whittaker drove, he began to have the feeling that something wasn't right.

He tried to shake the feeling off. He kept driving. The strange and inexplicable sensation grew. He thought that he ought to drive up to the Washington Street job and check it. He dismissed the idea. It meant driving six miles out of his way at the peak of the rush hour. Whittaker approached the intersection of Washington and Route 128.

Suddenly he turned.

He did not try to explain it to himself. He just turned.

Meanwhile, Jack continued to pray. It was the same simple prayer: "God, send someone." The bleeding in his nose hadn't stopped, and the blood ran down his throat and began to clot. "God, send someone." He spat the blood out, but it was getting more difficult. He wondered if it was dark yet. It seemed an eternity. Things were getting hazy . . .

Tommy Whittaker drove along Washington Street. The job was divided into two sections. He stopped his truck at a spot several blocks away from the cave-in, got out. He chatted with an engineer for the Metropolitan District Commission for 15 minutes. Whittaker did not mention the gnawing sensation that still would not leave him alone. The time was 5.45 p.m. It was still broad daylight . . .

Back in the trench, Jack struck some more arcs. He thought it might be dark now. He listened to the welder popping. He hoped someone would come, soon. The clot of blood in his throat was getting harder to bring up. He was a little surprised that he wasn't in panic.

Up above, a little way down Washington Street, Tommy Whittaker got into his truck, said good-bye to his friend, and started up again. The gnawing sensation, if anything, grew stronger. He reached a stop light. It was his turn-off to get back to 128 by a short cut. If he stayed on Washington Street, he'd have to go still farther out of his way. Tommy Whittaker braked his truck for a brief instant, then continued on.

Underground, Jack finally gave up striking the arc. It was making him breathe too hard. He didn't think he could last much longer. He couldn't get the blood clot out of his throat.

At that moment up above on Washington Street, Tommy Whittaker arrived at the spot where his friend was dying. Nothing seemed unusual. He noticed the stake-body truck. But it was a truck that Sullivan never used. Whittaker pulled up, got out of his truck, noticed the welder was running. He thought someone was inside the pipe, welding the inner circle. Nothing, still, struck him as unusual.

Then Tommy Whittaker saw the hand . . . the hand moved.

"Oh, God!" he whispered.

Whittaker jumped down into the trench and dug like a chipmunk with his hands. The earth was too packed. He scrambled out of the trench, looked back at the hand, shuddered. He shut off the welder and raced through traffic across the street to a garage.

Underground, Jack heard the pop-pop of the welder stop. It was then that he began to prepare to die.

Tommy Whittaker, feet away, shouted to the men in the garage. "There's a man buried alive over there! Get a shovel."

Back across the street Whittaker raced, carrying a snow shovel. He ran to the place where the hand stuck up, still not knowing it was his friend; he jumped down . . .

My brother, below, felt an extra pressure on top of his head. He knew someone was above him. He fought to keep from fainting.

Tommy Whittaker began to dig. He uncovered a wristwatch. He thought he recognised the watch band. He kept digging, until he uncovered the man's side. He saw the man was still breathing; the respiration was very weak.

Then Tommy Whittaker recognised my brother. Jack had fainted. Whittaker dug more frantically.

The rescue squad arrived. They applied an oxygen mask to Jack, while they were still digging him out.

Jack revived slightly when they put him on a stretcher. It was 6.30 p.m. "Who found me?" he asked.

"I did," said Whittaker.

With his lips, Jack formed one word.

"Thanks."

There was no more powerful word than that.

The gnawing sensation that had been bothering Thomas Whittaker went away.

Research for a Prayer

by PAUL DE KRUIF

Here's a well-known reporter who spent four years finding and perfecting his 'secret weapon' for living a better life.

ALL the first 40 years of my grown-up life I couldn't pray. Why? Simply because science could not prove to me there was any God to pray to. Then a man—for me he will remain miraculous—began to heal me of my worship of my own reason. Half-ashamed, I made a first attempt to pray.

Now, this has grown into a formal, yet simple, little prayer. Though the whole of it is brief enough, shorter bits of it can be detached for a quick block against this or that temptation. For me that makes it especially useful.

Often (not always) God answers. How do I know? By an instant feeling of what it's right to do, in a comfort of my conscience.

I can't give the full name of the man who played doctor to my sick soul; his first name is Earl. Humility, inherent in his religion, demands his anonymity. This was what I admired intensely in Earl, without having it myself.

As I got to know him bettter, Earl revealed a quality that's far from common. He had compassion. Few realise that compassion is sympathy translated into action. Earl had it.

Earl was only one of a strange army of over 100,000 of ex-doomed. He was an Alcoholics Anonymous, one of the very earliest—now 13 years post-graduate from the gutter.

Then Providence intervened for me. Senior Editor Marc A. Rose of the *Reader's Digest* asked me to look into a new chemical treatment for alcoholics. Here I was in my own bailiwick as a reporter of medical miracles. This news, if true, would be a sensation. There was no proven wonder drug at all for this dreadful malady.

My search showed the new treatment to be maybe, sometimes, somewhat hopeful. But it wouldn't work unless the victim would stay as bone dry as an Alcoholics Anonymous member. Earl (always ready to help me) saved me from my sometimes too eager enthusiasm for chemical wonders.

"What's your secret weapon?" I asked. "Only prayer," he answered. "We've got to ask a Higher Power to help us. We begin the comeback only when we *know* we can't help ourselves."

Earl explained that went for all of them, the whole miraculous hundred thousand of them. If they didn't pray —as some were too proud to—if they hadn't compassion to save other alcoholic downfallen—as some were too busy or too lazy to do—they were almost sure to slip back to destruction.

"You mean—you pray—to God?" I asked. This name I had used often, but only in profanity. Earl answered that he besought help from a Higher Power—not himself. Surely this prayer must be a mighty one, to save wretches from the gutter after medical science had failed. On the contrary, Earl's prayer turned out to be plain, even humdrum.

Praying, he simply said: "Help me to do the right thing in this situation—*Thy* will, not mine, be done." That was all—and every day, and in the dark of night, this was his sole defence against relapse into alcoholic doom.

For me, this was life's turning point. Though not alcoholic, I, too, lived in constant, deadly peril. As my own little God, all my grown-up life I'd struggled for the kind of *character* that Earl had superlatively. My brain—all the God I had—could distinguish bad from good. Yet, too often, I *did* the bad.

Now secretly I began to pray, telling nobody, not a living soul. For the first time in my grown-up life I said 'God' in a whisper, and not cursing. In trying to make a prayer, I turned professional. The writing man in me told me Earl's prayer lacked rhythm (as if that mattered!).

"God, help me *this* day to do what's right." There, that's got rhythm. Then I added—and it was the toughest thing I've ever had to say—"*Thy* will, not mine, be done."

That marked the beginning of a rugged battle against the big-I-guy in me that had so long misruled me, an almost four years of search, mostly in the dead of night, sleepless. It began by getting it clear what *not* to pray for—nothing material. Nothing that, by my having it, will deprive others. One bad night, getting nowhere, tired, half-awake, half-asleep—maybe dreaming, a small voice asked me—

What do you want that *all* can have?

For months I chewed at an answer. It was simple: I wanted God's help to be a better man, not a truly good man, only a bit better. Now came what seemed an answer. I quit trying to figure out, myself, how to be better. I kept stupidly, obstinately, asking God. His answer? It made me begin to drag out and dredge up and face my fundamental defects—I'd ducked this, lifelong.

What was one stymie in my fight to be better? Vanity. Having had some success as a writer, people patted me on the back and told me how good I was in there. I glowed.

"Help me, now, to fight vain thoughts." When praised, I began saying that to myself. I began to ignore the hoorahs.

In the night I began to give a hard look at my hypocrisy. Outwardly respectable, inwardly plagued by bad thoughts.

"Help me to think only what all may know." This was really a tough one, but I kept asking it.

Always these whispered cries for help were followed by—"*Thy* will, not mine, be done." And it was strange how this gave power to these bits of prayer.

One of my worst road-blocks in trying to be better was passing the buck to others, for my own mistakes.

"Help me always to blame myself." To this God answers most often, so far. This has had a queer dividend for others as well as myself.

"You are an alleged success," I told myself, "but how have you got ahead in life?" From the darkness came an answer, and not pretty. By hard work, but sometimes aided by a technique less admirable. I had been praised as a somewhat foolish, but big-hearted Otis. In the dark I reviewed the times this generosity was for my own advantage.

"Help me to give without thought of return." This now was added to the slowly growing prayer.

Never writing down any of it, continually forgetting or neglecting to use part of it. Many nights I tossed, and once Rhea, my wife, woke, asking me, "What's wrong?"

"Just working on that damn prayer," I answered.

So three years went by, and I began to feel different. Not mentally, but deep below my thinking brain.

And, praise God, conscience seemed a little stronger in me. At this part of the prayer I'd been working longest, "help me this day to do what's right." Yet here was the toughest of this discipline of self-examination. Was my conscience really strong? No—its muscles were flabby. What, in this gravest matter, to ask of God? This year came a simple answer—

"Help me to learn better what it's right to do."

This past summer I dared at last to join these fragments together, to set them down in a kind of order and with a rhythm that might make them easier to remember.

I looked at the prayer, read it over and over again. And this was eerie. It was as if I had not written it. I knew I had not written it. I felt cut down to size. I felt what my given name actually means. I felt—little.

Little enough to throw away what's past, to begin life over, to begin the exercise of everyday, not merely emergency, compassion—before recommending the practice of compassion to others. What is this little prayer? Only a rule of life that can't possibly be lived up to but *can* be struggled up toward.

I do not recommend anybody to follow this rule or even to try to remember it. This I believe: to come to grips with God, to bow down before His Will, to be constantly reminded of the need for His guidance, we should all try to make our own prayer. So here it is:

God, help me this day to do what's right—*Thy* will, not mine, be done
—help me to learn better what it's right to do; and then do it, no matter what the pain
—help me *now* to fight vain thoughts; and to think only what all may know
—help me always to blame myself; and to give without thought of return
Dear God—make strong my faith in Thee—*Thy* will, not mine, be done.

The World Is Waiting

by GENE LOCKHART

> *A distinguished actor searches his memories for a personal answer to the ageless question: "Where is God?"*

WHEN I was four my brother, myself and another boy were clearing the ice for 'curling', a game played in our native Ontario. While sweeping, the ice broke, and the three of us plunged into the freezing water.

A passer-by saw the accident. He quickly got a long pole and fished out our companion, who was so frozen and frightened he could not tell the man that there were still two other children under the ice. The man pushed the pole out again to retrieve what looked like the boy's cap, but it was the belt around my coat. He hauled me to the surface, and to the shore.

My brother drowned. I was thought dead. With frantic work it was hours before a sign of life appeared.

Later, while holding me in her arms, I heard my mother murmur, "Thank you, dear God, for being with him."

I was puzzled. "Where had God been? Where was He now?" Today, almost half a lifetime later, I have searched my mind and heart to reassemble the jigsaw pieces of yesterday—and to answer the question, "Where is God?"

God was certainly in the love my mother bore me when I first saw light. She loved people. For her no one could do wrong. If they did, she would find ample reason to prove it was not their fault.

No matter how empty our larder was, neither Mother nor Father could ever turn anyone away from our door. And many came. Mother loved the nearness of friends and children. At the least provocation she would stage a concert or a show in the town hall, or even in our own living-room, and almost always for children, from 7 to 70.

At the age of eight I started dancing with the famous 'Kilties Band of Canada', for which my father sang. Between engagements I received coaching in comedy from Harry Rich, who had another pupil at that time, my friend Beatrice Lillie. Today God finds in her His perfect instrument of laughter.

As I grew up and was preparing for a career on the stage, my mother advised me: "Arm yourself with another skill to take up the long intervals of searching for work."

At De La Salle College, I enrolled in a business course. Later I worked in the Toronto ticket office of the New York Central Railway, and then for the Underwood Typewriter Company. I am still wondering why I was hired. But the ways of the Lord are not our ways. He had something in mind.

The son of the president was Ernest Seitz, who became

my good friend and collaborator in writing songs. After my discharge from the Canadian Army at the end of World War I, we completed six songs. One of the songs was, 'The World is Waiting for the Sunrise'. That was in 1921 and I believe it is still a popular song to this day.

In one's heart there is always a God of hope.

At the age of 22 I decided to besiege New York. In due course my pockets were empty. I was too proud to write home for money, so I did what I had been taught from childhood: I got on my knees and prayed. A day later I was given a job installing a filing system for a milling company. While there I continued my studies, took singing lessons and knocked on many doors looking for stage work.

Then came a break—my first professional job in America —on a Chatauqua and Lyceum circuit. It lasted for 90 weeks. Since then, I have played an astonishing variety of rôles. The One who notes the fall of a sparrow has tempered me with a multitude of failures and humbled me with a small measure of success.

One of my successes was my marriage to Kathleen Arthur, an actress and musician of great merit in her own right. Shortly after our marriage we were twice blessed: I appeared in my first Broadway hit, *Sun-up*, which ran for two and a half years. We were given a lovely daughter, June. She began dancing in the Metropolitan Opera ballet school at eight. Today she is a television and stage actress.

There has always been a sweetness in the life and work Kathleen and I have had together that could only come through the guidance of a Divine Power.

Yes, He manifests Himself in actions large and small: in a helpful letter, a small service to another, an expression of sympathy, a sincere handshake. It may even be a simple: "Good evening."

One night in August 1933 I was walking down a New York Avenue when I passed one of the directors of the

Theatre Guild, head down, lost in thought. When I hailed him with a hearty, "Good evening," he looked up, but did not reply.

The Theatre Guild summoned me the next morning. After a reading I was assigned the part of Uncle Sid in Eugene O'Neill's tender comedy, *Ah, Wilderness*. The success of the play led me to Hollywood and the beginning of a long and happy career that still endures.

So, the God I know is a God of bounty and laughter, of hope and kindness, of testing and trusting. He is, above all, a God of mercy.

Fourteen years ago I went swimming off Laguna Beach, in California, and was caught in a fierce rip tide. I couldn't find bottom, nor could I struggle out of the undertow.

I had two thoughts then: First, I asked God's forgiveness. Second, I wondered how long the struggle would continue. I was sinking for what seemed to be the last time when a hand yanked me out. *He* was there again, in a watchful lifeguard.

Sometimes, before and after my skirmishes with death, I've forgotten to give thanks to the Saving Hand that swept me back to life. Thoughtlessly, I patted myself, egotistically praising my own luck, or vigour, or talent. Now I know. In each instance the circumstances of rescue implied intervention that was more than human.

The God of mercy was with me.

Inching slowly towards what is called 'Success', we are all restless with ambition. But, in my later years, as my thoughts turn to the end of my life, I know I have received, through the fire of time, a deeper sense of His power, a glimmer of the gentle way He moulds a soul. I have felt the touch of His sure hand in human friendships and in the eternal beauty of Nature.

Whenever one hears the song of a bird, the turning of leaves, the moving of waters, the silence of mountains, there is God.

In the agony of doubt, in the peace of mind, in the turmoil of life and in the peace of soul; in all of these there is God.

My life has proved to me that God is everywhere. I know now that the heart is ever restless, until it rests in God.